An Angel Among Us

A Story of Change, Brokenness and Reconciliation

Lawrence Balleine

Parson's Porch Books

An Angel Among Us: A Story of Change, Brokenness and Reconciliation
ISBN: Softcover 978-1-951472-68-9
Copyright © 2020 by Lawrence Balleine

All rights reserved. No part of this book may be reproduced or transmitted in any form or by any means, electronic or mechanical, including photocopying, recording, or by any information storage and retrieval system, without permission in writing from the publisher.

www.parsonsporch.com

An Angel Among Us

A Story of Change, Brokenness and Reconciliation

Introduction

An Angel Among Us picks up where the action of *Entertaining Angels* leaves off as Michael Lattimore, the chief character in both books, continues his summer sabbatical journey taking him to the dairy farm regions of Wisconsin. Michael, a social studies teacher, is seeking to determine how the changes in culture are affecting the family farm. On his way he meets numerous people facing a variety of circumstances. These lead Michael into interactions that he never could have foreseen prior to his departure. Whereas *Entertaining Angels* is a story of change, loss and healing; *An Angel Among Us* is a tale of change, brokenness and reconciliation.

The Fence Line

Michael did not quite slam on the brakes. But he slowed quickly. Out of the corner of his eye, he had caught a glimpse of something about two hundred feet ahead of him near the left side of the highway. A shade of tan, it had appeared suddenly and then quickly vanished.

A deer, Michael assumed. Although he was driving through an area where whitetails were plentiful, he still questioned why a deer would be out and roaming the fields at 10 A.M. But then he remembered that Elaine's – his wife's -- Toyota had been struck by a small doe while she is driving in the early afternoon. And when he arrived at the scene of Elaine's run-in with the deer and told her that deer only travel at dawn and at dusk, she had responded: "I guess this one didn't get the memo."

After a good visit with the Ericksons the previous day, a good night's asleep at the Hillview Lodge – a 1950's style motel with about a dozen units – and a hearty breakfast at Jim's Diner in Platteville, Michael was now on the fourth day of his sabbatical journey. Like the Willie Nelson song: He was "on the road again," proceeding along State Highway 81 a few miles northwest of Platteville.

As the breeze cleared the tall grass that had been obstructing his view, Michael recognized the moving object. It was not a deer, but a person, lying down and pulling at something.

Michael decided to stop. He veered on to the gravel shoulder. After taking a couple of steps out of his red Ford pickup, he quickly knew what the fella was doing: He was mending a barbed wire fence, a task that just about every farmer who pastures cattle must attend to from time to time.

"Hello there; can I lend you a hand?" Michael asked as he drew nearer to the fella wearing a tan Carhartt work jacket.

Looking up, the fella was a little surprised and said: "Thanks for the offer; but I'm just finishing up. Had to get this patched before I pasture my herd again in this field. A couple of them got out during the night, and we found them in the ditch on the other side of the highway. Almost had hamburger I didn't order."

"I'm Michael Lattimore."

"Good to make your acquaintance. I'm Jack – Jack Tollefson."

"If there's one thing cows are... It's that they are nosy. Always going somewhere, they do not belong," said Michael.

"Boy, isn't that the truth! So, you farm?"

"Not really," replied Michael. "I grew up in the country on about a half dozen acres in rural Manitowoc County. We were surrounded by dairy farms, so I got my taste of it."

"So, what brings you to this part of our lovely state?" asked Jack.

"I'm a social studies teacher from Green Bay and I'm actually on a trip around the state. I got a grant from a foundation to study the changing landscape of the Wisconsin dairy industry. I had lived in Ohio for nearly thirty years, but upon moving back to Wisconsin I noticed many changes to the farms I had been familiar with as a kid. Many of them were simply no longer active farms. So many barns and outbuildings were not in use. A lot less cows in the pasture. I remember a two mile stretch of one county road that had ten active dairy farms forty years ago; now only one dairy operation remains. But that one is huge. I imagine they must milk 1,000 head. I'm trying to find out how all the changes are affecting the small family farm."

"Well, that's me; operator of a family farm. Sounds like an interesting project. Maybe you could write a book detailing your findings or do a series of reports for Wisconsin Public Radio."

"I've never considered the public radio angle. I'll have to check into that," replied Michael.

Michael continued: "You've done a good job with the fence. That ought to keep your girls in."

"Thanks. Yeah, keep my girls in and the riffraff out. I only wish I could make the fence six feet higher and construct it using cinder blocks."

"Why's that? Neighbor problems?" inquired Michael.

"That's putting it mildly. Worst of all, he's not only my neighbor. He's my brother. It's hard to believe he and I came from the same parents. Growing up, Jake, that's his name, and I were different in so many ways. In school I played football, basketball and ran track. He was in the band. He was reading all the time while I was out in the woods huntin' or down by the river fishin.' A real Jacob and Esau story you could say. What we did have in common, however, was our love for farming. So, when Pa decided to retire, he split the farm right down the middle. Each of us got 160 acres and half of the herd of Holsteins – 45 head apiece. Mary and I got the original farm that my grandfather had settled on and Jake and Kathy got the old Sellmer farm that Pa bought back in the early 80's. Both properties are nearly identical."

"What about the machinery and the other equipment?" asked Michael.

"Most of that stayed with Mary and me and the kids on the home farm. But we got it all appraised – got a fair market estimate for what I was getting -- and I paid off Jake half of its value over the next eight years. Everything worked out well for a while. We would help each other with the crops and milked for each other when one of us needed some time off. It was all good until the accident. Then it all changed. The accident's been nine years ago, and we have not spoken since. In fact, come to think of it, it will be ten years ago tomorrow that we quit talking."

"Accident... What happened?" asked Michael, hoping he would not hear a tragic story like had the previous day at the Erickson farm. There he had learned of the car accident that claimed the lives of Joe and Linda Erickson's daughter, son in law and little granddaughter.

"You sure you want to hear about it?" asked Jack.

"I do, Jack," replied Michael.

Jack continued: "I remember it as if it happened yesterday. We were getting ready to put up the hay – second crop. I had cut and baled a twenty-acre field and it was time to pick up the bales, putting them on a flatbed wagon. We would always help each other with the baling. That morning he was to come over with his front-end loader. He would pick the round bales and put them on the wagon. I would drive the tractor and pull the wagon.

"When we baled at his place, he drove the tractor with the wagon, and I loaded the wagon using the front-end loader. Anyhow, he was supposed to show up after milking, but it was going on nine o'clock and he hadn't shown up. So, I decided to hitch the wagon myself. Usually, we did this together. But I was getting antsy, so I decided to do it myself. I had done this hundreds of times by myself, but it is something that goes smoother when you work together. I backed up the tractor close to the tongue of the wagon and thought I could easily drop the pin in the hitch. But as soon as I picked up the tongue, somehow the tractor slipped into gear and I got pinned. That is, my leg, crushed between the tractor and the tongue of the wagon.

"Thankfully, our son Andy who was still living at home at the time, was just coming out of the barn. He saw that I was in some serious trouble. He pulled the tractor forward and called 911. Who knows what would have happened if Andy had not come along just then? My leg was pretty mangled up, broken in two places. Some major bruises and a few gashes needing stitches. Had to spend over a week in the hospital. They feared infection. And then another six weeks going to rehab -- five days a week. Left me with this awful limp that I will have for the rest of my life. All because Jake didn't show up on time."

Michael continued to listen intently as Jack went on: "Finally, Jake shows up just as the EMS arrives. You know, if he had been there on time, it all would not have happened. We would have done the hitching together, just like we always had. But the lazy jackass was late. Sure, he apologized, but the deed was done."

"Sounds like it was a rough time for you," said Michael.

"That's putting it mildly."

After a brief pause, Jack continued: "You know all these Amish that are settling around here. I can't be like them."

"How so," asked Michael, assuming Jack would say something about their reluctance to use electricity and to live as folks now say, "Off the grid."

Instead, Jack said: "With their willingness to forgive."

The memory of an Amish community in Pennsylvania who so quickly forgave the killer of five of their girls at their schoolhouse flashed through Michael's mind.

Meanwhile Jack continued: "In fact, when Jake asked me if there was anything he could do, I told him exactly how I felt, saying: 'I ain't no charity case. We will get along OK. Andy will pick up the slack. So just mind to your own business.' So that's what we've been doing?"

"For ten years?" asked Michael, sounding flabbergasted.

"Yeah, actually ten years tomorrow. And you know what, I cannot say I miss him all that much. Our wives still talk, and the kids – the cousins – they get along fine, especially the youngest ones – their son James and our daughter Angie. They've been best buddies since they were little. They are only a year and a half apart. But Jake and me – we just don't speak to each other anymore.

"And you know what really fries my bacon?" asked Jack rhetorically, not expecting answer.

Michael could not help but remember yesterday's conversation with Joe Erickson who used the same expression. He wondered if it was a common one in this part of the state.

Jack answered his own question: "Jake keeps sending us Christmas cards. And he sends me a card for my birthday, and a card and to Mary and me for our anniversary. I feel like he's just rubbing it in."

"Did you ever consider that he might be trying to keep the door open for you two to get back together and restore your relationship?" Michael gently asked Jack.

Jack did not answer.

"If you don't mind me asking," Michael continued: "What happens when you see each other? Platteville isn't a big town and you're bound to run into each other every so often."

"Even though we go to the same church — when I used to go — and he and I were both there, and now if we see each other at the grocery store, we keep our distance. I think we have become quite good at this arrangement, if I can call it that. We must have, or we could not have kept it up for as long as we have.

"Speaking of church, about five years ago Pastor Thomson gave a sermon on forgiveness. I knew he was aiming it at me. He used the story where Simon Peter asks Jesus: 'How many times must I forgive my brother if he sins against me? Is seven times sufficient?' And then how Jesus replies to Peter: 'Not seven times, but seventy times seven.' I thought about telling Pastor to mind his own business. Instead, I just quit going to services after that, and I haven't been back."

Jack stood, leaned over and picked up his tools and continued speaking as he started limping toward his partly rusted Chevy Silverado. "St. John's Church has a different pastor now. Maybe I will have to check her out. I heard she is good with the older folks. And as you can see, I'm not getting any younger."

Michael followed a few steps behind Jack. As Jack arrived at his truck and threw his tools in its bed, Michael said with some trepidation: "Life passes by quickly. Jack, I hope you can get things worked out with your brother."

"Don't think that's gonna happen until hell freezes over," Jack replied.

"I'd like to talk with you more about your project, but I told Angie – she's fifteen and doesn't have her license yet -- that I would take her into town for her dental appointment. Gotta be there by 10:45."

"Oh, I certainly don't want to hold you up. Just one more thing. You probably ought not wear that jacket out here during hunting season. I first mistook you for a deer," warned Michael.

"Good reminder; thanks. Well, so long Michael, hope you have a good rest of your trip."

"So long," said Michael as Jack started his engine, put his truck in gear and drove off.

A few seconds later Michael was pulling off the gravel shoulder and back onto the pavement. He thought of his own children and expressed a thought of gratitude that Sarah and Simon, now young adults and out on their own, had gotten along well all through their growing up years and how they continue to e-mail each other a couple times a week. And he thought of his own siblings, Jennifer and Clark, and was glad for the good relationships he continued to share with them.

The Feed Mill

Michael knew that the feed mill was one place to find farmers. It is where they went to "shoot the breeze." They would talk about crops, milk prices, or give their opinion on the Brewers or Packers, and sometimes the Badgers. More than a little politics -- national, state and local – was often a part of their jabbering. That is why, when he saw a feed mill on the right-hand side of the highway, Michael stopped.

When Michael opened the screen door and stepped into the mill, two sets of eyes settled on him. Michael could read their minds: "Who are you? And what are you doing here?" So, Michael decided to answer the first of these non-verbal questions.

"Mornin' fellas, I'm Michael Lattimore."

Then Michael noticed a third fella bent over and sliding open a glass door on a cabinet next to the counter. He was securing a Snickers bar. When this fella turned, Michael could hardly believe his eyes. Five minutes earlier he had left Jack Tollefson and now he was here at the feed mill. Michael wondered: I thought he was taking his daughter to the dentist. How could he have beaten me to the mill? No one passed me since I pulled away after visiting Jack.

The fella with the Snickers bar looked toward Michael and was the first of the three mill occupants to speak: "Hi, Michael, I'm Jake Tollefson."

The mystery was solved, Michael concluded. This is Jack's brother. Not only his brother, but his twin brother; his identical twin brother. As Michael looked at Jake, Michael remembered something Jack had said about "coming from the same parents." Michael thought: Not only did they come from the same parents; they came from the same egg, both growing in their mother's womb at the same time. Yes, just as Jacob and Esau were twins and had a broken relationship lasting several years, the same kind of brokenness was being repeated thousands of years later by the Tollefson twins.

One of the sets of eyes who was standing behind the counter wearing overalls and a Rank Seed baseball cap – obviously the mill operator – lifted his arm and offered a friendly wave as he introduced himself to Michael: "Pete Samuelson; been here at the mill all my life. Are you new to the area?" he asked.

"No, just passing through."

"Passing through," said the second set of eyes that Michael had noticed when he entered the mill a moment earlier: "If you are just passing through, why would you ever want to stop here at the mill?

"Oh, by the way, I am Cliff. I've been coming here ever since I was 'knee high to a grasshopper' – first with my grandfather and then with my Dad -- and now it's just me."

"I know that if someone wants to talk with some farmers, the feed mill is the place to go," replied Michael.

"So, you stopped to talk with us?" asked Cliff.

"If that's all right with you?"

"Fine with me," said Cliff with Pete and Jake nodding in agreement. "We've covered our usual prattle and we need to hear something new from somebody new. Not often that someone drops in who we don't know. Take the stage my friend."

"Well, I'm actually spending a number of days driving around the state," Michael began.

"Must be nice," Cliff mused. "On vacation?"

"No; I'm a teacher."

"Oh, that explains it; you get summers off."

"Not exactly. I'm on a sabbatical."

"So, you're a college professor?" Pete inquired.

Jake was now seated in a green plastic lawn chair next to Cliff, while Pete remained standing behind the counter.

"No," said Michael. "I'm a middle school Social Studies teacher from Green Bay."

Then he began telling Jake, Pete and Cliff the same story he had told Jack about a half an hour earlier: "Upon moving back to Wisconsin after being away for nearly thirty years, I kept noticing all the changes that had occurred, especially with the family dairy farms, and so I wanted to do some 'on the field' research on the theme: 'The Changing Landscape of the Wisconsin Dairy Farm.' Thankfully, I received a grant from the Jefferson Foundation. It is covering most of my expenses. All they want in return is an accounting of these expenses and a brief report on my activities. That's no problem. I planned on doing these things anyway."

"Well Michael, what are you discovering?" asked Pete.

"I keep hearing the same stories: Stagnant milk prices, farmers selling their herds, some changing to raise beef cattle, competition from the factory farms, droughts, aging equipment and children who don't wish to take over the family farm – even when it's been in the family for well over a hundred years."

Pete reported: "I was just telling Cliff and Jake – just before you walked in -- that Fritz Hamlin is having to auction his herd of Brown Swiss. It's a cryin' shame. There has been cows on that farm since his grandfather operated it. In fact, he's the fourth farmer around here to stop milking cows since the start of the year."

Michael responded: "I've read that Wisconsin had somewhere around 100,000 dairy farms in the early 60's, and now that number stands at less than 10,000. About the same number of cows now as then – just a lot less farmers."

"Can you blame a fella for getting out of it, especially with milk prices continuing as they are? And it is plain hard work: seven days a week and milking twice a day. I can understand why the younger generation isn't keen on taking over their parents' farms, although I have hopes that James, our youngest son, will want to take over ours," said Jake.

"What might I be missing regarding the changes we're seeing on the family farm, or things impacting dairy farmers?" asked Michael.

"I'll tell you something else that's different – the women folk," said Jake.

"How's that?" asked Michael.

"Most of them work, but not necessarily on the farm. When I was a kid Ma drove the tractor, especially during haying season. She could milk cows as good as my Pa and she had a huge garden. She put up enough vegetables from the garden to feed the family well into the next year. And there were six of us – Ma, Pa, two girls and Jack and me. She always kept about fifty laying hens. When Ma and Pa went into town for the few groceries they bought, she took the eggs to the co-op for credit. And then they used the credit for something they could only get at the co-op. You hardly see that anymore -- a woman putting in that kind of time and work on the farm."

Meanwhile Cliff was leaning back in his green lawn chair and Pete – chewing on a piece of straw -- continued to stand behind the counter but was now leaning over with his elbows resting on the top of the old cash register. Both were nodding in agreement with their buddy, Jake.

"Like I say," Jake continued, "They're all working – well at least most of them work some place other than the farm. And they have got little time left over to help on the farm. I understand; after putting in eight or nine hours at work, they are tired. Take Kathy – my beloved of 40 years -- for the last thirty years she is worked at the Savings and Loan in town. She started out as a cashier; but has been the branch manager for the past dozen or so years. She carries the health insurance for us, and she earns a decent wage. Truth is, we could not make it on the farm income alone. And it's pretty much the same story with most other guys whose wives work."

"Couldn't have said it any better myself," responded Pete from behind the counter. "When I was a kid helping my Dad here at the mill, this was a busy place. But now – look at it – we have been here chewing the rag for what, nearly an hour, and my only customer has been you, Jake, getting your Snickers bar. Maybe I ought to turn this place into a candy, soda, and ice cream shop and call it 'Pete's Treats.'"

Pete made this statement with a fair amount of enthusiasm, causing Michael to believe that Pete had given serious thought to this major business change.

Pete continued: "Now that we've got the new biking and hiking trail crossing the highway ¼ mile back up the road, I maybe would have a steady supply of customers – at least during the summer. All I can say is, it is a good thing Paula has a full-time job as a teaching aid up at school. Her income really helps; and yes, we too, need her to keep working. She's the one with the health insurance the covers the two of us."

"Are you saying that getting health insurance is rather difficult to come by?" asked Michael.

"Well, you can get it, but for any decent coverage, it's real expensive. Jake and I are fortunate to have wives whose jobs provide family coverage."

"Sounds like you don't mind Kathy working outside the farm, Jake; and Pete that you're OK without having Paula to help you here at the mill?" inquired Michael.

"Don't mind at all. We consider their working in town a necessity, don't you agree Jake," asked Pete, not really expecting an answer.

Nonetheless, Jake nodded in agreement.

"Oh," said Cliff, "There's something else that's changed from when we were younger: politics. Use to be the politicians would talk about winning the 'farm vote.' Except for Buzz Jenkins, our assemblyman, I don't think any of them even know what the term 'farm vote' means."

"Hey, Michael, if you're so interested in what we farmers are all about around here, why you don't check this out," Pete said while pointing to a large poster on the wall behind the counter.

Michael moved in closer to see the poster. In bold letters, he read: "BARN DANCE." And in smaller letters: "Saturday night at the Jerry and Nita Nelson Farm. 6316 County Highway G. 7:30 to 11 P.M. Free admission. No alcohol. Celebrating Jerry and Nita's 50th Wedding Anniversary. Disc

Jockey 'Elvis' Schmidt spinning your favorite records from the 60's."

"Maybe I'll do that," said Michael, since I'm on no set schedule and have no other plans I must attend to. I have not been to such a shindig in fifty years. I grew up in Manitowoc County and with all the Poles and Czechs in that part of the state, dancing was a big thing. Lots of polka music.

"So, a barn dance. I can remember a friend from my high school days who would invite a bunch of us kids for a dance in the upper level of his barn. He'd do it every summer in late August."

Michael continued to share his memories: "Seemed that every country crossroad had a cheese factory, a Catholic Church and a tavern – usually with a dance hall connected to it. Most of the dance halls are now gone. When I returned to my home area after being away for all those years, well, that is another thing that had changed. Most of the taverns with their dance halls had either burned down or simply closed. Yes, another change to rural Wisconsin life."

"So, I'll see you there – at Jerry and Nita's place," asked Cliff, looking in Michael's direction.

"Count on it," said Michael.

Turning to Jake, Michael said: "Before I go, Jake, I need to tell you that I saw your brother Jack just before I stopped here. He was mending fence. Said he had a brother, but I never imagined a twin brother, and an identical one at that. That's why I may have appeared startled a bit when you turned to say 'Hello.'"

"Now there's a fella with a burr under his collar. At least you now got a chance to meet the nicer of the two," Cliff chimed in.

"Oh Cliff, don't be so hard on him," Jake said in return.

"You know, rumor has it that Jack's been mad ever since Andy graduated from the University with a degree in Animal Science and instead of coming back to eventually take over the farm or at least apply for a job around here, he takes off for Europe and works for an Ag tech company across the pond," reported Cliff.

"Maybe there's some truth to that, I really don't know. But I believe Jack will eventually come around," said Jake.

Turing back to Michael, Jake continued: "Yeah, Jack and I – we've got an interesting relationship."

"I picked up on that from my visit with Jack."

"I just hope you two will be able to work things out."

"How's he doing?" asked Jake.

"Only thing he mentioned was his limp. Otherwise, he seemed fine."

"Good to hear that," said Jake as Michael walked toward the door.

"Well then, until later," said Michael as he reached the door.

"Later," responded Cliff and Jake.

Meanwhile, Pete, still standing behind the counter said to Michael: "If you're ever this way again, don't be a stranger."

And with their farewells said, Michael made his way back to his pickup and said to himself: "If I'm going to a dance tonight I better head back into town and see if I can spend another night at the Hillview."

Within fifteen minutes Michael arrived at Jim's Diner for lunch. He enjoyed a bratwurst and home-made potato salad. The brat was OK. It just did not seem to have the flavor of a brat made in Manitowoc or Sheboygan County. I guess I'm just used to them being boiled in beer and onions before they are put on the grill, Michael reasoned. Or maybe it's just not the right combination of spices. None-the-less, the brat and potato salad were enough to satisfy his appetite.

Five minutes later he was back at the Hillview. He checked in and found himself in the same room he had occupied the previous evening. Must be their favorite room to rent out, Michael assumed.

He spent the next two hours documenting the mental notes he had taken from his conversations with Jack and the fellas at the feed mill. Recording extensive notes of his activities and conversations had become a daily ritual. He usually completed this task after he had checked in for the night. But, planning on going to the barn dance, he knew had had to complete this assignment before he left for the dance.

Then he took his sneakers off, found the TV remote, propped himself on the bed and started surfing the channels, stopping at the Brewers game. It was the third inning, and the score was knotted up: Cincinnati 3, Milwaukee 3.

He thought back to his childhood when the Brewers arrived in Milwaukee. He could not remember if it was 1969 or 1970. Somehow, a Milwaukee car dealer named Bud Selig lured the team away from Seattle where they had been known as the Pilots. Michael figured this name must have derived from a major employer in the Seattle area – Boeing aircraft. The team's new name was the Brewers. Michael reasoned, since Milwaukee had often called "The Beer Capital of the World," it was an appropriate name. Then Michael recalled how his Dad told him about the Milwaukee Braves who had come to

Milwaukee from Boston in 1953. His Dad had said that the Braves only stayed for a dozen years, pulling up stakes and relocating to Atlanta in 1965. Then he remembered his Dad's exact words: "Milwaukee is a good baseball town, and Bud Selig had the savvy to find a new team."

Although the Braves were successful, winning a couple of league titles and a World Series in 1957 with star players such as the great hitters Henry Aaron and Eddie Matthews, and pitchers Warren Spahn and Lew Burdette, the Brewers have yet to win a World Series. They had made it to the series once – in 1982 -- as the American League representative, but they were defeated by the St. Louis Cardinals, the National League champion. "Now, St. Louis," Michael thought, "Now there's a baseball town if there ever was one." Well, maybe this could be the Brewers year. They had played well over .500 ball in April and May. And they were doing well so far in June. "We'll just have to wait and see what the rest of the season brings," he mumbled.

The Barn Dance

Suddenly, or so it seemed to Michael, it was 6 P.M. Although he had not intended to do so, he had fallen asleep and had slept for nearly three hours. He was awakened by the sound of an eighteen-wheeler that pulled into Hillview's rather small parking lot.

"Gotta get ready for the dance – shower, dress, grab some supper, and then I need to find the Nelson farm,." Michael said to himself as he began to focus. "I recall seeing a sign for County Road G when I was on Highway 81 earlier today. I'll check there first."

Michael wondered what he should wear to the dance He pulled a fresh pair of jeans from his suitcase and found a red plaid flannel shirt he had stashed in his smaller canvas bag. Maybe it is a little bit too warm for this time of year, but he figured it would cool down as the night wore on. Then he topped himself off with a Green Bay Packers cap. It seemed that wearing his Packers hat gave him immediate credibility with those he was meeting on his journey around the state. Then again, maybe he was just imagining that.

Michael stopped for a grilled chicken sandwich and coleslaw at Jim's Diner and then was on the way toward the intersection of Highway 81 and County Road G.

Turning right off 81 and onto G, he located a fire number at the first farm: "N6060," it read. Just a little over ¼ mile to the Nelson place, he reasoned.

Within a minute Michael saw about forty vehicles parked in a freshly mowed field adjacent to a large red barn. He knew it was the right place. He pulled in, parked his pickup at the end of the second row of cars and trucks and started sauntering toward the barn. "This should be fun," he mused.

He walked up the ramp leading to the upper level of the barn. A few guests were entering the barn through the opening that had been created when the large sliding wooden door had been retracted. Michael joined them. After his eyes adjusted from the brightness outside to the relative darkness inside, Michael surveyed the interior of the barn. Although it was just after eight, it was still quite bright outside.

Looking about at the barn's rugged interior occupied by about eighty guests, Michael's his first thought was: "I have not seen so many cowboy boots in one place since I went to a rodeo in Cody, Wyoming years ago. They will just have to take me as I am – with my Nike sneakers." Placed around the perimeter of the dance floor, which looked to be about 30' by 30,' were several hay bales. Several folks were sitting on them. The bales were of the size Michael remembered from his youth.

Michael wondered if Jerry and Nita had not switched over to the much larger round or square bales; for all he had been observing on his trip were the much larger ones. Michael was glad to see the "old-style" bales; they were the kind he threw on a wagon pulled by his neighbor's John Deere back when he was a youth. Then there were seven or eight tables using bales for legs. The tabletops were 4'x8' sheets of 3/4" plywood that had been cut in half. He noticed there was room for four persons at each of the tables. Three of the tables were occupied. Each had two couples who were playing cards. "If this was happening at home," Michael thought, "they'd more than likely be playing sheepshead. But in this part of the state, it may be euchre or yass." He would have to move up a little closer and watch for a moment to determine which game they were playing.

He also could not help but notice all the NO SMOKING signs. They appeared to be tacked on every vertical pole. With the barn's wooden construction and the dry hay bales, it only made sense to ask folks to refrain from smoking. Attached to the rafters were several strings of small clear lights, providing ample lighting for the space. A beverage bar, surrounded by several coolers, was on the end of the dance floor to his left. And at the opposite end of the floor – to Michael's right – was a small set of risers that held the D.J.'s equipment. The sound equipment was vintage 1960's, right down to the Fender amplifiers and what Michael assumed was a Pioneer or a Garrard turntable. The D.J. – Wayne, whose stage name was "Elvis" – was nowhere to be seen. Michael assumed he was taking a break.

"Hey Michael," a voiced called out from across the dance floor. It was Cliff from the feed mill. Taking a circuitous route around the back side of the hay bales that formed a ring around the dance floor, Michael made his way to greet Cliff.

"I see you made it. Obviously, found the place OK," said Cliff.

"Sure did."

"Can I get you something to drink? Soda, iced tea, lemonade; or I think they've got some bottled water." inquired Cliff.

"Sure, I'll go with an iced tea, and no sugar please," replied a grateful Michael.

"Comin' right up."

When Cliff went to the bar, Michael could not help but think: If this barn dance was being held on a farm around Green Bay, there would be a keg or two somewhere within easy access.

A moment later Cliff returned: "Just like you ordered; an iced tea with no sugar," Cliff reported.

"Thank you, Cliff."

"Let's find a seat at that table over there," Cliff said, while pointing to the last empty table – the farthest one from both the dance floor and "Elvis'" amplifiers.

As they reached the table, suddenly Jake Tollefson appeared, and Cliff offered him one of the two vacant folding chairs. It was odd that they had not seen Jake come into the barn; for in a small town everyone looks to the door when someone arrives. It is just the way it is. But with the sliding door opened for the evening, there was no opening and closing of the barn door, and thus no sound to attract attention. So, folks were slipping in with few taking notice.

"Hello, Jake. Long time no see." Michael said jokingly.

"Michael, I'm glad you could make it."

"OK," said Michael, "So we've got Cliff and Jake. I suppose Pete will show up, too."

"No," reported Jake. "He and Paula were going to head over to Dubuque to visit their daughter and her family. Pete said they'd be leaving right after he closed the mill at 4 o'clock."

Wayne "Elvis" returned from his break and announced the next dance: "Grab your partner and get out there on the floor. This is 'Hang on Sloopy' – a hit that reached No. 1 on the U.S. Billboard Hot 100 list in 1965." In his mind, Michael pictured Terri – a high school classmate – dancing her heart out to "Hang on Sloopy."

Returning to the present, he noticed about eight couples, led by a smiling pair who Cliff identified as Jerry and Nita, make their way to the dance floor.

Michael was glad that they were able to secure the table that was the farthest away from the two Fender amplifiers. For he, Cliff and Jake were still able to carry on a conversation, despite thee rather loud 60's rock 'n' roll favorites that Wayne was spinning.

"Is your wife here?" Michael asked Cliff.

Immediately Jake lowered his head and gave Michael a look that caused Michael to realize he had asked the wrong question.

Cliff however, interjected, saying to Jake: "It' OK. It's been three years." Then, looking at Michael, Cliff continued: "I lost Grace three years ago in spring. She was a fine woman – a wonderful partner and a good mother to our kids: Edward, Lucy and Travis. Breast cancer. We thought it was in remission, and I suppose it was for a while, but it returned with a vengeance. Tried some additional chemo and radiation, but it had metastasized and invaded her whole body it seemed. Just took her down to skin and bones.

"Worst four months of my life. But she got her wish. She died at home in her sleep. And she was able to say 'goodbye' to the kids the previous day. Knowing her time was short, they were all home for the weekend. Edward came in from Madison, Lucy from Rockford, and Travis got an emergency leave from the Air Force and flew in from down south somewhere – I do not remember exactly where.

"She lived up to her name. I always say that my Grace was full of grace. She always saw the best and brought out the best in everyone; and she 'never let the sun go down on her anger.'"

Jake interrupted: "You describe her well. Grace – full of grace – that's a perfect description of this wonderful woman we all knew and loved."

"Thanks Buddy."

"I'm sorry for your loss," said Michael.

"Thank you. I am doing OK. Some days harder than others. The kids have been great. They check on me more than they need to. The two older ones are married and have kids of their own. '" You've got their own families to look after,' I often say to them. Nonetheless, I am grateful for their care and concern.

"One thing that really helped me was something Grace told me about a week before she passed. She told me about how Gracie Allen – you're old enough to remember her I am sure – left a note for George Burns, her husband. It is a note George found shortly after Gracie's death. The note said: 'Never place a period where God has placed a comma.' I think what Gracie was telling George and what my Grace was telling me was to not give up after my death – like it is all over – a period. Rather, consider this rough time to be more like a comma, for there will be more ahead for all of us."

"Cliff, that's beautiful. Thank you for sharing that with us," said Michael.

"Yes, Cliff," said Jake, "I've heard you tell this story many times, but it never grows old."

"Enough of me," said Cliff.

Then he turned to Jake with a request: "Jake, why don't you tell Michael about your family?"

"Yes, Jake, I'd be glad to hear," said Michael.

"Well," said Jake, "I better tell the truth because Kathy – my wife – is standing right over there. See the two women standing next to the stage. That is Kathy on the left and her good friend Susan on the right.

"Kathy and I were high school sweethearts. We met in band. I played the trombone, and she played the sax. Our friends called us: 'The Brass Duo,' although we seldom played duets."

While Jake was speaking, Michael noticed Jake's twin brother, Jack, enter the barn. He was accompanied by two women. Michael assumed one to be Jack's wife, and the other appeared to be much younger – perhaps his daughter. Michael could not help but wonder what would happen if Jack and Jake crossed paths. But then he remembered how Jack had said they had learned to keep their distance. Michael assumed: Rather than outward animosity, it is more like giving each other the "cold shoulder" – a shoulder that seemed to have become "frozen" over time.

Focusing again on Jake, Michael heard Jake go on: "We got married a couple of years out of high school and have three kids – just like Cliff: Darlene, John – named after his Uncle Jack -- and James. Darlene, our oldest, always did extremely well in school. She received a slew of scholarships at the close of her senior year in high school and was able to go to Ripon College and graduate debt-free. She started as a biology major, but about halfway through she felt led in a different direction.

"Pastor Thomson had a big influence on her, especially while she was in confirmation class. Anyhow, about half-way through college, she began to wonder about the ministry. Well, when she graduated from Ripon with a degree in psychology and with high honors – I might add – she was admitted to the Divinity School of Vanderbilt University. Again, scholarships enabled her to attend such a top-notch school. After getting her Master of Divinity degree she was ordained and served a congregation in rural Minnesota for four years, but then decided to return to Vanderbilt to work on a PhD. in ethics.

This summer she is working with a program called: 'A Christian Ministry in the National Parks.' She's at Acadia Park on the coast of Maine."

"Are you still planning on going out to see her?" Cliff asked.

"Yes, Kathy and I are hoping to make it out there sometime in August."

"Good for the two of you," said Cliff.

"John, our middle child – like Cliff's son – has been in the Air Force. Been in for about six years. He always dreamed of flying as a kid. When he was plowing or harvesting or doing something else out in the field, he would often put the tractor in neutral, and gaze up in the sky to stare at some jet streaking overhead. More than once I had to tell him: 'Get your head out of the clouds' Then he would say: 'I wonder where that jet is coming from and where it's going.' We must be in some sort of flight zone, because there are a lot of jets that fly over. Suppose many are going to O'Hare. Well, now he's gotten his chance to fly.

"And then there's James. He is what we call our 'oops' child. Did not think we would have additional children after John. One of each was simply fine with us. But then, lo and behold, Kathy is expecting again – at age forty. We worried a little about Down's Syndrome, but James was and is simply fine. Same thing happened with Jack and Mary. They thought they were "one and done" after Andy weighed in at just over eleven pounds, but about twelve years later here comes Angie. Anyhow, our James just finished his junior year of high school.

"He continues to be a big help on the farm; and yes, I am hoping he will take it over some day. He is here somewhere tonight. Oh, I forgot, he asked to borrow the keys to the Chevy. He said if his cousin Angie shows up, he and she would probably take off for the Dairy Queen for a while. Living next door to us, he and Angie were inseparable playmates. They are not only cousins, but they continue to be best friends. They're always looking out for each other."

"Sounds like a wonderful family and Jake, I hope you get your wish," said Michael.

"What wish is that?"

"The one you mentioned not only just now, but also this morning at the mill; that James will take over the farm someday."

Cliff chimed in: "I'm sure he'd be a loyal costumer at the mill, just like you are, Jake. That is, if Pete does not transform the place into Pete's Treats. Well, come to think of it, if James likes Dairy Queen he'd probably like Pete's Treats, too."

"What about you, Michael?" asked Jake. "You told us this morning about your travel and your summer project; but what about your family? And do they still call Green Bay, 'Titletown,' and do you get to many Packers games?"

"Well, I am blessed to have a wonderful supportive wife who encouraged me to take this sabbatical journey. She is a teacher, too. She is teaching remedial reading this summer. Elaine, that's her name. We have been married for 28 years and have two kids – both grown and "out the nest." as they say. Sarah is married and works in Milwaukee for a non-for-profit agency that helps low-income folks secure decent housing. Simon, like Elaine and me, teaches – third and fourth grade. He is married, too. And they live in ..."

Trying to build suspense, Michael paused for a moment and then looking directly at Jake, said: "They're living in Ripon."

"Any grandchildren?" asked Cliff.

"No, not yet."

"When they come, it will be wonderful. They're the greatest blessing of growing older," confided Cliff.

"Oh, and yes, Green Bay is still called Titletown," said Michael in response to the second question. "They got that name back in the 60's when they won so many titles under Lombardi. Evidently, the name was not heard too much when they were having their bad seasons. But once they won the Super Bowl to close out the '96 season, you started hearing it again. And no, I do not get to many games. Season ticket holders have them all locked up. You can sometimes find some for sale on Stub Hub or some other secondary seller. But you pay a hefty price for them; usually around three times their face value. So, we're easily talking 150 dollars or more a pop. You know they have sold out every game since the early sixties. And there are thousands on the waiting list for season tickets. It's just nuts."

Michael felt he had said enough and finished by saying: "It's been a pleasure to share these things with you."

Time passed quickly as Michael enjoyed the company of Cliff and Jake. He found himself tapping his foot to the oldies that "Elvis" was playing. The music ranged from Skeeter Davis' – "The End of the World" to the driving beat of "I Can't Get No Satisfaction" by the still famous Rolling Stones. "Elvis" even played one of Michael's favorites: "Don't You Care" by the Buckinghams.

Soon "Elvis" announced: "One more record before we take a break. It is another slow one, this time from 1968. Jerry and Nita, will you lead us?

Soon the mellow harmony of the Vogues and their classic hit -- "My Special Angel" – filled the air as nearly twenty couples followed Jerry and Nita to the dance floor.

As soon as the last lyrics of the Vogues ballad were sung, most of the folks in attendance were eager to step outside and into the cool summer evening. The barn had grown rather hot and stuffy over the past couple of hours.

Jake excused himself, saying: "Well, Cliff and Michael, I'm gonna see what Kathy's been up to, and see what James and Angie's plans are."

A moment later a tall, smartly dressed muscular fella – about nineteen or twenty -- walked into the barn and headed straight toward the bar. Cliff noticed him right away and leaning over to Michael said: "Here comes trouble."

The young man approached the fella tending bar and in a loud voice demanded: "I'll have a Bud Light."

"I'm sorry, Tony, this is a dry party – no alcohol." said David Totter, the evening's designated bartender.

"Bull! I want a beer," Tony demanded in an even louder voice.

By now the action at the bar had caught the full attention of the remaining fifteen or twenty folks in the barn, including Michael and Cliff.

Tony barked: "You call this a party? What the hell kind of party is this with no beer?"

Just then Jerry strode over to the bar and gently asked: "Do we have a problem here?"

"Of course, we have got a problem," replied Tony, "He won't give me a beer."

An Angel Among Us

"I'm sorry Tony, we're not serving any beer tonight."

Then David offered his observation: "Tony, it seems like you've already had enough for the night."

Hearing this, Tony completely lost his temper and turned-on Jerry, giving him a hard shove and saying: "Maybe you ought to stay out of this old man; all I want is a damn beer?"

Tony had hardly finished his lament when Harv Ware and Tom Greenup – two of Jerry's neighbors – both good size young men in their thirties and former high school wrestling state qualifiers – appeared on the scene. They took hold of Tony under his armpits – one on each side -- and dragged him out the door as the onlookers cleared a path.

Cliff, taking a deep breath, looked over to Michael and reported: "I'm not surprised by all this. That Healy boy is one mixed up young man. Cannot say it is all his fault. His stepfather is in the penitentiary for assault and battery. His mother abused drugs and alcohol. Judging from Tony's age, it was about twenty years ago when she got pregnant. Rumor says it was a one-night stand. To this day no one knows who Tony's real father is.

"His Mom, if I remember correctly her name was Debby, got clean for a while but then got hooked on crack cocaine. Then she died of some sort of overdose when Tony was about twelve. He lived with his stepfather until his stepfather was sent to prison. For the past year or two, he has been renting an apartment over the pharmacy. He quit going to school the day he turned sixteen but got a job as a detailer at one of the automobile dealerships in town.

"Everyone around here knows about Tony. Some feel sorry for him. Some try to reach out to help him. Some are afraid of him – for obvious reasons. Most just try to ignore him and hope he will just go away. I am not surprised at the way he is turned out. I'm afraid that someday he'll kill himself if he doesn't kill someone else first."

Shaking his head, Michael responded: "Such a sad story. Are there any resources out there to help him?"

"Yeah, all kinds of them, but he refuses to make use of any of them. I suppose it will take something drastic before the court system will finally intervene and demand that he engages in some pretty extensive psychotherapy," replied Cliff.

While all this was going on Jake had located Kathy, and they had walked to just outside the large sliding barn door. Their son James had also hooked up with his cousin, Angie, and were now finally on their way to his parent's Chevy Impala to go to the Dairy Queen. It was about 9:15 P.M. and the Dairy Queen was open for another forty-five minutes. The cousins were almost to the car when Tony, driving an old beat-up Ford Ranger, whipped around the end of a line of vehicles and stopped directly in front of Angie and James.

Tony got out of his truck and threw a sucker punch at James. He connected with James' right eye. Immediately, James fell to the ground. Angie began to scream as Tony grabbed her, saying: "You're coming with me!" as he forced her into his truck. Intending to stop Tony, James staggered to his feet. Wobbling for a second or two, James slumped back to the ground.

Angie's screams had caught the attention of everyone outside the barn, including her Uncle Jake's. Meanwhile Tony put his truck in gear and started to make a bee line to the main driveway and exit.

Suddenly the sound of a sickening thump filled the air. Jake had jumped in front of Tony to stop him, and he was struck by Tony's truck. Tony stopped for a brief second – just long enough for Angie to make her escape -- and then Tony hit the accelerator and sped out of the driveway and onto County Highway G.

Meanwhile the stunned crowd seemed frozen in their places. James regained his footing and rushed over to his Dad. Jake was conscious, but in obvious pain. Thankfully, Cy Sanger – one of the nearly fifty or sixty who had witnessed it all -- immediately called 911 on his cell and reported the emergency.

Kathy rushed to Jake and bent down and said: "Honey, we're going to get you some help right away." Then she broke down and put her head on Jake's shoulder and pleaded: "O Jake, please be OK."

Maybe Jake was in shock or maybe he just did not want Kathy to worry, so he responded: "Don't worry, Kathy, it's just a scratch." That is what he always said when he had done some bone-headed thing around the farm and ended up with stitches.

Meanwhile Angie, her flower print top partially ripped from her tussle with Tony, was running back toward the barn. She was screaming: "Daddy, Daddy."

Duane Simmons called out to her: "I think your Mom and Dad are still in the barn."

Those inside the barn had not heard the commotion outside because Stan Smith had decided to pull out his harmonica and play the three songs he knew. A very patient group of ten or fifteen folks who were still in the barn politely listened and applauded each tune.

Sobbing all the way and running up the ramp and into the barn, Angie spotted her Mom and Dad where she had left them moments before. As she reached her Mom and Dad, she could barely speak: "Uncle Jake, he's been hurt. Daddy, you have to help him."

"Why would I want to do that? As you know, we're not exactly on speaking terms."

"Listen Daddy," said Angie – her voice now clearer: "Uncle Jake saved me; he rescued me."

"Saved you? What are you talking about?" asked Jack.

"Tony hit James and then wrestled me into his truck. As he was starting to get away, Uncle Jake jumped in front of him and Tony ran into him. I think he might be hurt bad. You've got to help him."

Jack and Mary walked briskly out of the barn and joined the others who had gathered around Jake. By this time, some were hugging Kathy, trying to give her the support she needed. Others knelt close to Jake offering words of encouragement: "Jake, you hang in there." "We've got your back." "Help is on the way." Sarah Jones knelt off to the side. She was praying.

Mary pulled away from Jack and walked over to comfort her sister-in-law, leaving Jack standing alone. He appeared to be in another world. He did not know what he should say or do. He just stood there, staring at his twin brother. It was as if he was looking at himself as he flashed back to his own accident of nearly ten years earlier.

Meanwhile, Michael and Cliff had moved to the entrance of the barn. Michael surveyed the scene, taking note how small-town folks come together when one of their own has been injured. Cliff excused himself saying he was going over to talk with a couple of his neighbors he spotted in the crowd.

Michael, now standing alone, reflected: "One-minute Jake, Cliff and I are talking and enjoying each other's company, and the next minute Jake is seriously injured. Life can change so quickly, especially on a farm – although this could hardly be classified as a 'farm accident.'" He could not help but think how it must have been for the Ericksons – the couple he had visited yesterday – who had lost three loved ones in an instant.

Michael noticed Jack standing alone, about ten feet from Jake. He felt led to go to Jack.

As Michael made his way to Jack, the sirens from a County Sheriff's Department squad car and the EMS vehicle could be heard growing louder and louder each passing second. Within another minute they arrived on the scene. A sheriff's deputy got out of her cruiser and began moving the cooperative crowd back to the ramp leading to the entrance to the barn so the EMS crew could attend to Jake. She knew the whole Tollefson clan. She allowed them to remain close to Jake. They only had to stand back a little way and not get in the way of the EMS attendants. Michael remained at Jack's side. He could see Jake responding to the questions of the emergency squad. Jake was conscious, but each time he moved, he winced.

Meanwhile the crowd watched nervously as the EMS personnel checked and re-checked Jake's vitals, and started an IV drip in his right arm. Then one of the EMS team members flashed two fingers in front of Jake's face, asking him: "How many fingers do you see?"

The EMS team carefully put Jake on a stretcher, secured him tightly, and loaded him into the back of the EMS vehicle. The EMS crew chief walked over to Kathy and gave her a hug.

"Yes," thought Michael, "It's a small town. Everyone knows everyone." He listened closely as the crew chief reported to Kathy: "At this point things look encouraging. But we need to transport him to the hospital to get him thoroughly checked out. We know his right leg has been severely injured; and it appears like he might have suffered a concussion."

"But his life is not in danger?" Kathy asked, eagerly awaiting a response.

"Thankfully, it appears that his life is not in danger," said the crew chief.

"O thank God," Kathy said, with a few tears of tentative relief filling her eyes.

"Do you have a way to the hospital?" asked the crew chief.

"Yes, my son James is here. He'll take me in."

"Just park in the lot near the Emergency Unit, and when you come in the lobby, there's a desk there with an attendant. Dottie is on duty. She'll direct you from there."

"Thank you. Thank you so much," Kathy responded.

Then the crew chief and the rest of the EMS team climbed into their vehicle. One sat in the driver's seat and another beside him in the passenger seat and two – including the crew chief – crawled in the back with Jake. The vehicle slowly left the field where all the dance party guests had parked. Then the ambulance sped up a bit when it arrived at the much smoother driveway. And when it turned onto County Highway G, the driver stepped on the accelerator and turned on the siren.

The crowd continue to gaze at the ambulance until it passed over a rise and both its flashing lights and siren began to fade.

Then the sheriff's deputy, who had been assisting the EMS crew, stood and faced the gathered group. After identifying herself as officer Nancy Morris, she made a request: "Did any of you witness what happened here?" At least forty hands shot up. The look on her face indicated that the deputy was surprised by the larger number of witnesses. She continued: "I'll need some of you to stop by the sheriff's department on Monday morning so we can take your statements. Do I have any volunteers?" Again, several raised their hands. "O.K. Thank you. Another deputy will see you on Monday morning." Officer Morris did not ask for their names. She was confident they would show up.

The deputy said so long to the group, returned to her cruiser, got in and pulled away. No siren this time.

Jerry and Nita stood at the top of the ramp at the entrance to the barn and Jerry called out: "Well folks, there's not much we can do out here. Jake is in good hands. Let's go back inside and see if we can have some more fun." Nita learned over to whisper in Jerry's ear. Jerry nodded, and then continued his announcement: "Meredith, our granddaughter, is here from California and she has made the most beautiful anniversary cake. I'm guessing she is cutting pieces as I speak." With that said, the crowd began to filter back into the barn.

Michael, still standing with Jack, turned and said to him: "You know I met Jake at the feed mill after I left you this morning. I thought for a moment he was you, until he introduced himself as Jake, and I realized he was your brother. You failed to mention that you and he are twins – identical at that. Then I had another chance to visit with him and Cliff tonight.

"Yeah, I saw you guys at the table over in the corner," said Jack.

"Almost feels like I should go to the hospital and check on him," said Michael.

And then Michael, feeling an impulse, asked: "Jack, do you want to come with me?"

"I don't know if I should. I saw Mary and Angie pull out a moment ago. They were following Kathy and James. She left without telling me. But I suppose that's what I deserve for what I said back in the barn."

"Was it something that bad?" inquired Michael.

"Oh, I just started running my mouth off again when Angie came in to tell me that Jake was hurt."

"Why don't you come with me and show me the way to the hospital?"

Michael did not tell Jack that he already knew the way. He had noticed the sign for the hospital when he arrived in Platteville the previous evening.

Jack was silent for several seconds. Finally, he said: "OK. I guess it will be alright since you don't know where you're going."

"It's settled then. Just give me a minute," said Michael, "I'd like to say, 'so long' to Cliff."

Michael located Cliff in the barn. He was on the dance floor with an attractive middle-aged woman. Observing Michael looking at Cliff and his dance partner, Duane Simmons – who had seen Michael and Cliff sitting together earlier – tapped Michael on the shoulder and reported: "The woman Cliff is with? That's Judy Waller. She lost her husband about the same time Cliff lost Grace. She just retired after teaching English for thirty- five years at the high school."

The Hospital

Michael and Jack climbed into Michael's pickup for the five-mile trip to the hospital. For the first two miles they said nothing. Jack finally spoke, as if mumbling to himself, but still audible to Michael: "Do you suppose the Lord can ever forgive me for the way I've treated Jake?"

"What are you trying to say, Jack?""

"I'm saying I have been a real jerk. I have been blaming Jake for the accident all these years. It wasn't his fault. It was mine. I should have waited for him to help me. I just got impatient. On top of it all, I learned later why Jake was late that morning. It was because both John and James had caught some sort of bug and he and Kathy were up most of the night taking care of them. That is why he got a late start milking his cows, and that's why he was late getting to our place."

Seeking to give Jack some needed reassurance, Michael replied: "Jack, your question about the Lord forgiving... I can only say that when Jesus was about to be put on the cross, he asked God to forgive them. He did not say who the 'them' was. It could have been the religious aristocracy who put him on trial; it could have been Pontius Pilate –the Roman governor -- who handed Jesus over to be crucified; it might have been those who were carrying out his execution; or maybe Jesus meant all of them. All I can say is, if the Lord was willing to forgive like that, yeah, I think the Lord can certainly forgive you."

"I sure hope so."

Again, they rode in silence for the next few minutes until Jack told Michael to turn left onto the hospital's long driveway. The sign at the entrance read: "Regional Medical Center."

Quite a complex for a rather small town; but I suppose it serves a large area, Michael reasoned.

Jack limped alongside Michael as they entered the waiting area just outside of the emergency room. There sat Kathy and James, Mary and Angie.

Jack asked, "Any news?"

"Not yet," answered Kathy. "I'm glad you're here, Jack."

"Thanks to Michael," Jack replied. Then facing Mary, Jack added: "This is the fella I was telling you about; from this morning when I was fixing the fence."

A moment later the four EMS attendants who had come to the Nelson farm to help and transport Jake walked out of the Emergency Room. Three went outside while the crew chief stopped at a small writing desk in the corner of the waiting room. He pulled a spiral notebook from his backpack and began writing. Michael assumed he was probably filling out a report on the call he and his crew had just completed. Meanwhile, the three other EMS personnel made their way to their vehicle that was still parked just outside the automatic sliding doors.

A loud beep sounded. It was coming from the waistband of the EMS crew chief. He punched a couple of numbers into his cell phone and listened intently. Then he quickly gathered his notebook and hustled out the door. You could hear him shout to his partners: "We need to go. Another call just came in. Vehicle accident out on Highway 81 by the Schneider Bridge." And in a flash they were gone.

Kathy was disappointed. She had hoped the crew chief might have been able to bring them some news on Jake's condition.

A moment passed and the clerk, seated just outside the door leading to the Emergency Room, answered her phone. A few seconds later she said: "Thank you. I'll tell her."

The clerk – Dottie Harrison, stood up from her chair and addressed Kathy: "You can go up and see your husband. He's just been moved upstairs to Room 237."

Kathy and James led the way to the elevator, followed by Jack, Mary and Angie. Michael decided to stay in the waiting room.

Upon getting off the elevator on the second floor, the five Tollefsons walked about forty feet down the hall. Spotting Room 237, they entered just as the emergency room doctor -- who had accompanied Jake to his room – was about to leave. He turned to those coming into Jake's room and was startled upon seeing Jack. Then he realized that Jake had an identical twin.

Since the hospital contracted with a group of E.R. physicians based in Madison, the doctor did not know the Tollefsons.

"I'm glad you're here. I am Dr. Sorensen. Is one of you Jake's spouse?"

"I'm Kathy, Jake's wife," Kathy responded: "And these are all family members."

"Can I share with you what we know is going on with Jake? And is it all right if the rest of the folks hear what I have to say, or we can go to a small conference room by nurse's station – if you prefer more privacy?"

"Like I said: 'We're all family.' It's OK for all of us to hear your report," responded Kathy.

"The x-rays indicate that Jake's right leg is broken in two places: one break is in the femur, that's the big bone extending from the knee up the thigh to the hip joint. And the tibia is also fractured – about halfway between the ankle and the knee," said Dr. Sorensen leaning over and indicating the location of his own tibia. "He might have a slight concussion. Doesn't seem too severe. And so far, there has been no indication of internal injuries. And we don't expect any. Oh, and it looks like there may be a couple of cracked ribs. They didn't show up on the initial x-rays, but sometimes they don't appear until the next day or two. Obviously, Jake is here for a few days."

Dr. Sorensen took a breath and then continued: "You need to know that we've already talked to Dr. Glaser, the orthopedic surgeon, and we've scheduled Jake for surgery tomorrow morning. We need to pin those fractures".

"You're doing this on Sunday?" asked Kathy.

"Yes, the sooner the better."

Then, looking to the group of Tollefsons, Dr. Sorensen asked: "Do any of you have any other questions?"

No one asked any, but each of them replied: "Thank you, Dr. Sorensen."

Dr. Sorensen left the room saying, "I've got to get back to my duties in the ER. If you need me, I will be there until 6 A.M."

After the doctor left Jake's room, Kathy, who had walked to Jake's bedside, leaned over to give Jake a kiss on the cheek.

Jack quickly moved closer to Jake's bed. He could no longer refrain from speaking: "I'm here to apologize, Jake. I have been an absolute jerk. All these years of blaming you for my accident. It was not your fault. It was my bone-headed stubbornness and impatience. Jake, can you ever forgive me for being such a pain in the you know what?"

"Do you really mean it or are you just afraid you may have lost me tonight?"

"Well, honestly, both."

All eyes in the room were now fixed on the two brothers and the drama that was unfolding.

"Of course, I forgive you Jack."

Tears now filled the eyes of Kathy and James, and Mary and Angie. They were tears of joy and relief.

"And to think that we could have lost you tonight," Jack said. He began sobbing, releasing tears that he had suppressed for years.

"Lean in here Jack," said Jake.

Jack moved closer and Jake reached up to give his brother an along overdue embrace.

"You know, Jack, if we had waited with this for another hour or two, we could made it to ten years. Thank God we didn't. We've got to make up for lost time," Jake whispered, but loud enough for everyone in the room to hear.

"If there's anything I can do, Jake, just ask," said Jack.

"Well, you'll be sorry you asked. The girls don't milk themselves. James would probably appreciate some help."

"Of course, I'll help," said Jack.

James reached over to squeeze Angie's shoulder as Jake asked Jack: "Do you think I'll end up with a limp like yours? Then they really won't be able to tell us apart?"

The room filled with laughter.

Kathy asked Jake: "Are you in much pain?"

"No. They gave me something down in the ER and the pain isn't bad. I'd give it a two or three on a scale of one to ten."

"That's good, Uncle Jake," said Angie.

"Jake," said Jack, "I've got to ask: Whatever possessed you to jump in front of Tony?"

"I know -- there's a fine line between bravery and stupidity. But I guess it was just a reaction. When I saw Tony hit James and then grab Angie, I knew I had to stop him. I was afraid of what Tony might do to her. I love that girl with all my heart," said Jake, looking at Angie. "Remember, she's our God-child and we promised to look after her."

Jake's response brought more tears to Angie's eyes.

Seeing Jake yawning, Kathy said: "Well, Honey, you've been through a lot. You probably need some rest. I'll be here in the morning. James will come after milking and chores, won't you?" she said while turning to James.

"Of course, I will," said James.

"It's late, but I'll try to get a hold of Darlene and John when I get home; or else I'll call them early in the morning to let them know what's going on."

"And we'll come right after I get home from church, won't we Jack," offered Mary.

"Our course, Mary."

"Good night, Dad," said James.

"Good night, Son."

Good night Uncle Jake," said Angie.

"Sweet dreams, Pumpkin," said Jake. It was a name he had called her since she was a little girl with a head full of curly orange colored hair.

"See you tomorrow," said Jack and Mary.

"Until then," replied Jake.

"I'll be here as soon as I can in the morning, Honey," said Kathy. "I'll call the nurses' desk early and make sure I get here before they take you in for your surgery."

"Good night Sweetheart --- sweet dreams." said Jake.

The five left the room not knowing if Michael would still be in the ER waiting area. As they got off the elevator and approached the waiting room, they saw Michael in the same plush chair he was sitting in when they left him a half an hour earlier. It appeared that he had not moved since they had gone up to Jake's room.

"You're still here!" Jack said with some surprise.

"I wanted to get a report on Jake before I left. I'm leaving town in the morning and I wanted to make sure he's going to be OK before I go."

"Jake's going to be alright," said Mary. "Broken right leg – in two places; possibly a couple of cracked ribs, and maybe a slight concussion. He is gonna have surgery on his leg in the morning to put a couple of pins in. But all in all, he should be OK."

"Thank goodness," replied Michael.

"Thank you so much for caring," said Jack. "And I need to tell you: Jake and I are OK. I finally did what I should have done years ago. I apologized and we finally got things patched up. Thank you for helping me through this."

I don't know what I did,." said Michael.

"You listened to me. You did not judge me even though you could probably see that I was the one in the wrong. You cared enough to bring me here. And you reminded me how fast life passes. It all helped."

"Thank you, Jack, but it was nothing."

"You might think it's nothing, but it means more to me than you'll ever know," said Jack.

Michael looked at the group and continued: "Well, it has been more than a little exciting down here in the ER since you left. The EMS returned, bringing in somebody from the accident on Highway 81. From the looks of the faces on the staff, it must be pretty serious."

Just then the door leading to the ER flew open and Officer Morris, the sheriff's deputy who had earlier been at Jerry and Nita's farm, walked out.

Seeing the Tollefsons, she reported: "I probably shouldn't be telling you this, but you'll find out soon enough. It's the Healy boy, Tony. Since he was involved with the hit and run in with Jake, I think you should know. Evidently not long after he left Jerry and Nita's he headed out on 81. He hit the Schneider

Bridge. From the looks of his pickup, he must have had it floored. He was not wearing a seat belt. Someone he had passed a minute earlier came upon the scene and called us immediately. We found him on the bank of the creek. Funny thing is, even with all the lights from the EMS vehicle, we could not locate any skid marks leading to the place of impact. Either his brakes went out or..."

Deputy Morris cut herself off mid-sentence, and then added: "I shouldn't be speculating. I've probably already said more than enough."

"Is he going to be alright?" asked Kathy.

"God only knows. He's in bad shape. They've got him stabilized to the point where they're getting ready to move him to the Intensive Care Unit," said Deputy Morris.

"Wow," all the Tollefsons and Michael responded in unison.

Then Deputy Morris went over to the same small writing desk that the EMS crew chief had used only an hour earlier.

The five Tollefsons – Kathy and James, Jack and Mary and Angie said their goodbyes to Michael and expressed their appreciation for his kindness. Michael held out his hand and shook each of their hands. And soon they were all headed out of the hospital parking lot.

Michael checked his watch and noticed it was nearly 11:30 P.M. As he made his way to the Hillview, he thought: "It's unfortunate that it takes a tragedy or a near tragedy to get folks back together. But better late than never, I suppose." Then he thought: "As soon as I get back to the Hillview, after I talk with Elaine to check in with her for the day, I'm calling Jennifer and Clark just to see how they're doing. I'm glad they live on the west coast. It is only 9:30 there. I know they'll still be up."

The Next Morning

Kathy arrived at Jake's room just as a nurse – who identified herself as Sam -- finished putting an I.V. into Jake's left wrist in preparation for his surgery.

"Can't say I like this thing, but I appreciate it, "said Jake to Sam as she prepared to exit his room.

"He's all yours," Sam said to Kathy as Kathy stepped into Jake's room.

"Hello Sweetest thing in the world," Jake announced to Kathy.

"Well, aren't you chipper this morning!"

"I should be. I've already had a dose of the 'happy juice.'"

"James will come after he gets finished with chores. Jack came over earlier to help him with milking. Then James went over to help Jack with his," Kathy reported.

"Jake, I've got some good news," said Kathy. "I got through to Darlene and John right after I got up. I figured they would both be up, especially Darlene with all her Sunday morning duties. Darlene said she would try to come home. She said that her program allows its participants five days off at some point in their twelve-week term of employment. She assumes that her supervisor would probably let her have a few days if she finishes her obligations with the two ocean side worship services that are planned for later this morning. But then, here is the good news: She just called back as I drove into the hospital parking lot to say she could come home and that she was able to get a reservation. She's flying from Bangor to Chicago later this afternoon, and then she'll rent a car and hopes to be home by midnight."

"Kathy," said Jake, "Darlene shouldn't feel like she has to come home for this. Remember, all of this is just a scratch."

"She said I couldn't talk her out of it no matter how hard I tried. And you and I both know that special bond between a father and a daughter. I've known it since the day she was born."

"Well, it will be good to see her," said Jake.

"Yes, it will."

"And John, how's he doing?" asked Jake.

"He said he's got a ten-day mission coming up – starting tomorrow. He asked if you had your cell phone, and I told him you did. So, I assume he'll be calling soon."

A knock sounded from the door and standing there was a woman who introduced herself: "Hi, I'm Connie Greene, the hospital chaplain. May I come in?" she asked.

"Yes, by all means," answered Jake.

Walking up to Kathy and standing beside her, the chaplain said: "Rough night last night I hear."

"You wouldn't believe it," replied Kathy.

Turning to Jake, Connie, who was wearing a clerical collar, asked if there was any way she could be helpful.

"I don't think so," said Jake.

"Are you ready for your surgery?" she asked.

"I guess I have to be. Don't seem to have any other choice," said Jake.

"Well, may I share a prayer with you?" the chaplain asked.

"That would be fine."

Connie held both Jake and Kathy's hands and offered a prayer asking for guidance for Dr. Glaser and the surgical team; for Jake to be granted patience during his recovery period; and for a lessening of any anxiety that Jake and Kathy may have been experiencing. She closed by praying: "We place Jake and Kathy into your tender care and ask that you fill their hearts and minds width an assurance of both your presence and your abiding love. Amen."

Chaplain Connie then squeezed Jake and Kathy's hands firmly and said she would stop by later in the day; and with "thank you's" from Jake and Kathy, the chaplain left to continue her early morning rounds.

As soon as the sound of Chaplain Connie's footsteps faded, Jake had another visitor. It was Dr. Glaser who came by to introduce himself, and to ask if either Jake or Kathy had any questions.

"No," they both replied simultaneously, and then Kathy added: "Dr. Sorensen did a good job last night telling us what needs to be done and explaining things to us."

Dr, Glaser went on: "I'm pleased to report, Jake, you suffered no internal injuries. The radiologists continue to rule out any broken ribs. I think by now you would know if you had any; you would be feeling them. And your concussion – if you have one – is mild. Any headache at all?"

"No," said Jake.

Kathy thought of a question. "How long will Jake be in surgery, Dr. Glaser?"

"Looking at the x-rays and knowing what we're dealing with, I would estimate about two hours," responded Dr. Glaser. "Any other questions?"

"None from me," Jake replied.

"I can't think of anything else," said Kathy.

"OK then, we should be all set. See you Jake, in just a little while. And Mrs. Tollefson, I'll stop to see you when we're all finished and give you a report."

As soon as Dr. Glaser left the room, Kathy said to Jake: "Jake, you wouldn't believe what happened after we left you last night. As we went back through the emergency waiting room we ran into the Deputy Morris. She was the one who came out to Jerry and Nita's place. She had gotten back from another call – an accident west of town. A pickup truck slammed into Schneider's Bridge. Evidently, it was going way over the limit."

"Oh, don't tell me, Tony?" asked Jake.

"Yes, how did you know?" responded Kathy.

"I just sensed it when you started talking, and when you said pickup truck – I was even more certain."

"Sounded like he's in pretty rough shape. Deputy Morris said he was being moved to the ICU. Jake, evidently his injuries are pretty severe."

"I was afraid something like this was going to happen."

Just then they heard a sound echoing from the hall. Jake and Kathy looked toward the door and recognized the sound's source. The cart that would take Jake to surgery appeared in the doorway. As the stainless-steel padded gurney entered

Jake's room, the attendant who was pushing the cart introduced himself: "I'm David, your designated driver, and I'm here to take you to surgery. Are you ready, Jake?"

"Guess it's now or never," replied Jake.

"Come to think of it, they played that at the dance last night," said Jake.

"Played what?" asked Kathy.

"'It's Now or Never,'" said Jake as he smiled at Kathy.

"Oh, with everything that's gone on, how would I remember that?"

David pulled the gurney right next to Jake's bed and adjusted both the bed and the gurney to that same height and then asked: "Jake, can you tell me your full name, date of birth, and what kind of surgery you're having this morning?"

Jake replied, "Jacob Henry Toleffson, February 9, 1956; and I'm getting pins put in my broken right leg – in two different locations."

"Nailed it, or should I say, 'pinned it' – no pun intended," said David, while he carefully transferred Jake onto the gurney.

Then, turning to Kathy the attendant said: "You can wait in the surgical waiting room down on the main level. It's just to the right as you come in the main entrance. Dr. Glaser will want to talk to you when he's done with the surgery. He'll look for you there."

Kathy leaned over and gave Jake a kiss on the cheek and said: "I love you. Jake."

Jake responded by saying: "I love you, too. See you in a little while, Honey."

Kathy stepped out of the room so it would be easier for David to maneuver the gurney. As the attendant raised the gurney's side rails, Jake made a request: "Can you take me to Tony's room in the ICU? I need just a word with him."

The attendant knew that it was Tony who ran into Jake the previous evening, and he was concerned what Jake might say or try to do, so he first offered an excuse: "I'm just subbing this morning for Bob Sturgis. He's usually on duty on Sunday mornings. I don't know if I'm allowed to do what you're asking."

"If you don't tell, I won't either," replied Jake. "Please, it's the least you can do for someone who's about to undergo surgery."

"Well, I suppose, but for only a minute. They're waiting for you in surgery."

The Intensive Care Unit was just a short distance down the hall from the operating room. David maneuvered Jake into the ICU, got permission from Tony's nurse, and wheeled Jake as close as he could to Tony's bed. Tony was hooked to all kinds of equipment, his arms and face were swollen, and he remained in in a coma.

"Tony," Jake began, "I don't know if you can hear me, and I don't know what's ahead for you, but I want you to know: I forgive you, and I'll be praying for you."

And with that said, Jake nodded to his attendant and they made their way to the surgical unit.

A couple of hours earlier Jack had gotten up at his usual 5 A.M. and had driven next door to Jake and Kathy's. As he stepped out of his blue Silverado he heard the side door to Jake and Kathy's house open and close. It was James, sporting a purple right eye, courtesy of Tony's sucker punch delivered the previous evening. After saying "Good morning" to each other, they entered the barn and headed for the milking parlor. They were greeted by sixty milk-laden Holsteins, already lined up and wanting to be relieved of their "white gold." That is what James called their milk.

Jack and James did not say much to each other but listened to the soft music from the local F.M. station. All the Tollefsons believed that their cows milked better when the music was playing. "Our girls are more cooperative and give more milk when the radio is on; but it's got to be tuned in to our local station," both Jake and Jack often said.

After they finished milking Jake and Kathy's herd, both Jack and James – Jack in his pick pickup and James in a four-wheeler -- headed over the Jack and Mary's place where they milked Jack's herd. When they finished, James returned home to feed the calves and do his other chores.

Jack, however, did something he had not done in nearly five years. Instead of tinkering around with something in the machine shed, he went back in the house and took a shower. As he stepped from the bathroom he was greeted by Mary.

"Jack, what on earth are you doing? You scared me," said Mary.

"What's it looks like? Can't a man take a shower in his own house?"

"Yes, but what on earth for? You never shower this early in the morning."

"Church!"

An Angel Among Us

"Church?" Mary inquired; her voice filled with surprise. "You're going to church today? You've not been to church in years. "

"I've been telling myself that I should finally go and meet Pastor Ann. She's been at St. John's for nearly three years now and I hear she's quite attractive."

"Is that any reason to go to church?" chided Mary.

"I suppose not, but I'm still going. I suggest we quit our chit-chat and hurry up so we're not late."

Jack, Mary and Angie arrived at St. John's at about 9:20 for the 9:30 service. As they walked from the parking lot to the front door of the church several folks crowded around Angie to ask how she was doing. News travels fast in a small town and many had heard about the incident the previous evening at Jerry and Nina's place. Reaching the main entrance of the white frame church building, Bernie Sievers, one of the ushers, saw them and said: "Welcome folks. Good to see you, Mary and Jack and Angie, too." Then looking directly at Angie, he said, "We're all glad you're OK."

The prelude started and Jack, Mary and Angie made their way to their usual places in the seventh row from the front on the pulpit side. It is where they sat ever since Jack and Mary were married in St. John's in 1978.

When the prelude ended and the acolytes had lit the altar candles, Pastor Ann entered from the sacristy and announced: "Grace be unto you and peace from God our Father and from the Lord, Jesus Christ." And the whole congregation responded: "And also with you." Then Pastor Ann invited those who were able to stand. The service continued with a call to worship, an opening hymn, and a time for confession. Pastor Ann announced: "Hear these words from the first letter of John: 'If we say we have no sin, we deceive ourselves, and the truth is not in us.'" Pastor Ann and the congregation then continued with a prayer wherein a confession of sins in thought, word and deed were admitted. After the prayer of confession, Pastor Ann returned to the lectern to offer a declaration of pardon, saying: "My friends, hear this good news. We are reminded further in John's letter: 'If we confess our sins, God who is faithful and just will forgive us our sins and cleanse us from all unrighteousness.'"

Again, just like five years ago, Jack felt the pastor was directing the words squarely at him. But instead of being outraged, he felt comforted. And he knew in his heart that the Lord had forgiven him.

Michael was right, he said to himself, not only did the Lord forgive his accusers and executioners at the time of his crucifixion, but he also forgives me. And yes indeed, he said to himself, what Pastor Ann said a moment ago is right on target: "This is good news, good news indeed."

Pastor Ann stepped to the middle of the chancel and announced: "This morning our special music is presented by Meredith Smythe. Meredith is the granddaughter of Jerry and Nina Nelson, who, as you all know are celebrating their 50th wedding anniversary this weekend. In honor of this occasion and I might add – glorious accomplishment – Meredith will be singing one of Nina's favorite songs. It was made popular by the group, 'Alabama,' some years ago."

Meredith stepped up from her place in the third pew where she had been sitting with her grandparents and stood where Pastor Ann had been standing just a few seconds earlier. Jack and Mary looked at each other as if to say: "I recognize her from the party last night." Then, singing without accompaniment, Meredith began with the refrain: "Oh I believe there are angels among us -- Sent down to us, from somewhere up above -- They come to you and me, in our darkest hour -- To show us how to live, to teach us how to give -- They guide us with the light of love."

As Meredith sang, Jack thought about the past twenty-four hours: "Michael appeared to me yesterday – just out of the blue. And he kept showing up just at the right time. Never judging me, but listening to me, reminding me that 'life is short,' and then inviting me to accompany him to the hospital."

Meanwhile, Meredith was nearing the end of the last verse: "They wear so many faces, show up in the strangest places – To grace us with their mercy, in our time of need."

"Could it be that Michael is one of those angels Meredith is singing about?" Jack pondered.

Meredith completed her solo and Jack got comfortable in his pew. Putting his arm around Mary, he was more ready than he had been in years to hear the scripture texts and Pastor Ann's sermon.

At about the same time James was helping Jack with his herd, Michael had gotten up, showered, dressed, checked out of the Hillview and made his way to Jim's Diner. He took his usual seat at the counter. The waitress – the same one who had waited on him for his first three visits – walked to within a few feet of Michael. Then she leaned over slightly and after saying "Good morning," she asked Michael: "What is it now, four times in a row? You're like my regulars. I'm about ready to consider you one of them."

"I think I've lost track, of how many times," replied Michael as she handed him a menu.

After finishing an order of pancakes and sausage, Michael headed over to St. Joe's for mass. Although he was not a

Catholic, Michael enjoyed the pageantry of the mass and the rather formal liturgy. He recalled that in high school, most of his buddies were Catholic, and he would periodically attend services with them. Plus, St. Joe's offered the earliest church service in town. If he wanted to go to church and get an early start with his travel, St. Joe's was the place to go.

A part of the service at St. Joe's were the prayers of intercession. Included in these were prayers asking for healing for both Jake and Tony, although neither was a member of the St Joe's Parish. Not only did Michael experience some surprise that the news concerning Jake and Tony had already made it to the ear of the local priest, but he also found it commendable that prayers were being said for those outside the parish. Then he assumed: "This is a small town; everybody knows everybody." But he also sensed that as Fr. Frank was offering his prayer, the folks at mass were genuinely concerned about Jake and Tony.

Fr. Francis' homily was right on target, thought Michael. He spoke about the worth of every individual, saying: "Each of us has worth, because each of us is a child of God." Michael reflected: Yes, even the Tonys of this world.

At the completion of the mass, Michael got back on Highway 81 to continue his journey toward the Mississippi River. He soon passed the field where he had met Jack about the same time the previous day. He thought about their conversation, and how he had connected with him later at the dance and recalled their time riding into the hospital. Then he passed through the intersection of Highway 81 and County Road G and thought about everything that had happened last night just up County G at the barn dance. Then he passed the feed mill where he had met Jake, Cliff and Pete. And a moment later he came to a bridge. He somehow knew it was the bridge that Tony had hit. Just as Deputy Morris had said, there were no skid marks leading up to the big black smudge at the corner of the bridge.

Michael wondered how both Jake and Tony were doing. He recalled what Cliff had said about Tony: "I'm afraid that someday he'll kill himself, if he doesn't kill someone else first." After Michael had proceeded over the bridge he looked in his review mirror and whispered: "Whew! What a day and what a night! I don't think I've ever had another like it."

Suddenly Michael felt compelled to turn around and go back. For some unknown reason he knew he could not leave Platteville – not just yet. The Mississippi River can wait, he said to himself. Something was telling him that the folks he had met yesterday were not through with him. He turned around at the next driveway and headed back toward the town he had left moments earlier.

Later Sunday Morning

"Trust your instincts," Michael's high school coach had said to him on many occasions' years ago.

Michael preferred to call it: "Paying attention to the nudges." Early in his teaching career Michael began to realize if a particular student entered his mind and lingered there, there was often something going on in the life of that student – something that needed attention. Sometimes it was a student's failure to grasp the material Michael was teaching. Sometimes it was something going on in the student's home life. Sometimes a student was struggling with anxiety or depression. Sometimes it was trouble with peers. Sometimes it was something else. Whatever the "it" was, it often called for some sort of intervention. Thus, Michael knew that whenever he was experiencing some sort of nudge or impulse, he needed to pay attention to it. And that is what he was doing. He had just experienced some nudges, compelling him to head back to Platteville.

This was not the first time he felt such nudges. The same thing had happened to him a couple of days earlier when he felt compelled to stop at the Erickson farm. There, the Ericksons invited him to share supper with them. This was followed with a heart-felt conversation. Unbeknownst to Michael, their post-supper visit helped the Ericksons "work through" some of their unresolved grief resulting from the tragic loss of their daughter, son in law and granddaughter.

"Evidently, there are some loose ends I need to tie up," Michael said to himself as he arrived back in town. Just then he noticed the blue sign with a large white H. He knew instinctively one thing he needed to attend to: Check and see how Jake Tollefson fared during the night.

As Michael parked his red pickup in the hospital parking lot, he noticed a rather discreet entrance to the building. He may not have noticed it had there not been a black Chevrolet Suburban parked in the driveway leading to the door. The Suburban – with its darkened windows -- was backed up to the door. "That's gotta be a vehicle from a funeral home," Mike thought. Seeing the vehicle caused Michael to worry if something unforeseen had happened to Jake during the night.

He hustled into the hospital. He remembered the emergency room clerk's instruction last night: "They're moving Jake to Room 237." Michael decided not to wait for the elevator. He ran up the stairs to the second floor and walked briskly to Jake's room. He peered in. Jake's bed was empty. "Please tell me 'no,' it can't be," Michael muttered to himself. "Sounded like he was doing all right when the family left last night. I wonder if something unforeseen arose in the night."

A CNA was walking past Michael, and seeing the distraught look on his face asked? "Are you looking for Mr. Tollefson? He's still in surgery."

"Whew," Michael breathed a sigh of relief; for he realized that the vehicle he had seen – if it was from a funeral home -- was not there to pick up Jake.

"His wife is down in the waiting room on the first floor," said the CNA.

"Thank you very much. You've been a big help."

Michael took the elevator down to the main floor. Looking to his right he saw a sign for the surgical waiting room. When he arrived, he saw it was occupied by one person – Kathy.

Looking up, Kathy saw Michael approaching and she asked: "What are you doing here? I thought by now you'd be long gone."

"I started out; got about six or seven miles out on Highway 81, but then got a feeling I needed to come back. So here I am. Any word on Jake?"

Kathy responded: "No. He's been in for a couple of hours. I'm hoping to hear something soon."

"I hope so too," said Michael.

Kathy then changed the subject of the conversation: "I suppose you haven't heard. Tony died a little less than an hour ago."

So that is the reason for the Suburban parked at the discreet entrance, Michael figured.

Kathy continued: "He died without ever regaining consciousness. I overheard some of the cleaning staff talking about it when I went for a cup of coffee in the cafeteria."

Michael experienced another nudge. Although he did not know why, Michael felt that – if possible – he should stay for Tony's funeral.

"It's a shame. What was he, nineteen, twenty? So much life ahead of him," said Michael.

"Yes, a short life; but a very difficult and troubled one," replied Kathy.

"Still too young to die."

"I fully agree," said Kathy. Then she reported, "On the brighter side of things, our daughter Darlene is coming home. Hopes to be here by midnight."

"That's great. I'm sure you're excited to see her," replied Michael.

"I sure am and so is Jake."

A moment passed and the hospital volunteer that Kathy had "checked in" with just before going to the waiting room stuck her head in the door and announced: "Mrs. Tollefson, Dr. Glaser just called down to my desk. He said the surgery went well and he'll be here to report to you in a few minutes."

"Thank you," said Kathy, and then gazing upward she added: "And thank you, Lord."

"That's good news," said Michael.

A couple of minutes passed while the two of them reviewed some of the previous night's events. Then Dr. Glaser appeared. He was still wearing his green surgical scrubs. Although he had been the orthopedic doctor for the hospital for the past three years, Kathy and Jake had never met him. That is, not until earlier in the morning when he had popped into Jake's room to introduce himself. As he entered the surgical waiting room, both Kathy and Michael stood to greet him.

"This is our friend, Michael," said Kathy to Dr. Glaser as she introduced Michael.

The surgeon extended his hand saying, "Nice to meet you."

Michael replied: "It's a pleasure to meet you."

"Michael's been a real God-send for us. Like an angel, he keeps showing up just at the right time and in the right places," Kathy eagerly told Dr. Glaser.

Michael thought: Wait until I tell Elaine about this; being compared to an angel. She'll never believe it.

"Sit down please, please," said Dr. Glaser. Then sitting on a wing-back chair opposite them, Dr. Glaser began his report: "Jake did fine during the surgery. We just got started on him a little later than we expected. We had a little hold up in the surgical ward. I was able to do the pinning right where we had hoped."

Dr. Glaser pulled out a small sketch pad. He flipped to its first page. It showed an image of a human skeleton. Then, with a fine line marking pen, Dr. Glaser indicated where he had inserted the pins into Jake's leg. Then he continued: "Jake should be fine, but we need to keep him here for at least a couple more days to make sure everything checks out OK – post surgery. Then he'll have at least a month of physical therapy. But I think you already knew that. He can come into the hospital rehab unit for that. He won't have to stay here. He will only have to be here about an hour each time he comes. We'll talk more about that before he's released."

"So, when can we go up and see him?" asked Kathy.

"He'll soon be out of the recovery room. I assume the staff should have him settled back in his room in about fifteen minutes. Feel free to go up then."

Dr. Glaser left and Michael checked the time: 11:15.

"That's a relief," said Kathy. "After all the trauma last night, I was afraid how Jake's body would react to the surgery. But I guess he's a tough old farmer."

"Now let's hope the recovery period goes as smoothly as the surgery," replied Michael.

Just then James walked in. He quickly acknowledged Michael and then asked his Mom: "How's Dad?"

"Out of surgery. Dr. Glaser just reported that all went well. We'll be able to see him in just a little while."

Kathy, James and Michael's conversation turned again to the events of the previous evening. When James asked Michael about still being in town, Michael replied: "Well, I left earlier this morning, but then I felt I needed to come back. So here I am."

"James, there's something I need to tell you," said Kathy in a very somber tone: "Tony passed away. Apparently he died a little over an hour ago."

"Oh, that's too bad. I never really knew him, but always felt kind of sorry for him," said James, even though his right eye remained swollen from the punch he had taken from Tony the previous evening.

Their waiting time was soon over, and Kathy announced; "How 'bout we go up and see your Dad?"

"Sounds good, Mom," said James.

"How about you, Michael?" asked Kathy.

"You two go first. I will wait here a while. You all need some family time. I'll be up in another 15 or 20 minutes."

Kathy and James made their way to Jake's room. Reaching Room 237, Kathy tapped on the door.

"Come on in," Jake replied.

Kathy and James entered and were surprised to see Jake much more alert than they expected. Kathy went to Jake's bedside, bent over and kissed him on the cheek.

"Dr. Glaser says everything went fine in surgery but to expect to be here at least a couple more days."

"I figured as much."

"Then they'll be some therapy," said Kathy.

"Yeah, from what they said last night, that is no surprise. I kind of remember Jack's post-surgery routine," replied Jake.

"James, it looks like Dad and I are going to be expecting a lot from you this summer. Are you up for it?"

"'You know I am. With Uncle Jack helping, we should get along OK. Plus, it is summer vacation, so I've got the time."

Looking to James, Jake said: "Mom told me that Jack already helped with the milking this morning,."

"He did. We worked well together; I suppose it was kind of like the old days before you two had your 'falling out.'"

"I couldn't be any happier that we got things patched up."

"Oh Jake, Michael is down in the waiting room," reported Kathy.

"What's he doing here? I thought he'd be long gone by now."

"I did, too. He started out but was evidently only out of town a few minutes when he had a feeling he needed to return. And so, he did," replied Kathy..

"James, would you mind going downstairs and getting him?" asked Jake.

"Sure Dad. I'm on it."

As soon as James was out of the door, Kathy turned to Jake and said: "I've got some sad news. Tony did not survive his injuries. Never came out of his coma. He died about 10 o'clock this morning."

"I'm sorry to hear that," said Jake. "I'm glad I was able to have a word with him just before my surgery."

"You spoke with him?" asked Kathy incredulously.

"I did, briefly."

"Could he talk? I thought he was in a coma," questioned Kathy.

"Even though he was in a coma, I still said what I felt I needed to say to him."

"And what was that Dear?"

"After I told him that I didn't know if he could hear me, I said to him: 'I forgive you.'"

"Jake, you're such a good man," Kathy responded.

James reentered his Dad's room. Michael followed immediately behind James.

As soon as Jake saw Michael, he said the Michael: "My word, I thought you'd be long gone and half-way to Lacrosse by now."

"I thought so too, but I got down the road a bit and decided that I ought to come back."

"So, I hear. I suppose you just don't want to miss any excitement like there was last night," Jake said jokingly. "And if that is the case, Michael, I need to tell you – last night was an exception. Even with all the college kids in town during the school year, the kind of stuff that went on last night is pretty rare."

"Honestly, I don't know what drew me back. Just felt I was supposed to."

Michael then approached Jake's bed, reached out and shook Jake's outstretched hand: "How are you doing?" Michael asked.

"Right now, feelin' no pain."

"Good. Let us hope it stays that way."

"Listen, Jake, I just wanted to stop in to see how you are doing. I'll go so you can visit with Kathy and James. I think I'll be in town another couple of days, so I'll stop by tomorrow."

"That will be just fine. I look forward to it," said Jake.

Michael left Jake's room. On his way down to the main floor, he decided if he was going to stick around town for a while, he better gets a room at the Hillview for another couple of nights.

When Michael stepped outside, he noticed that the black Suburban had left. Michael figured that it must have been at the hospital to pick up Tony.

Michael got in his pickup and found his way back to the Hillview. He entered the motel office and was greeted by the friendly desk clerk: "I didn't think we'd be seeing you again. Did you forget something?"

"No. Actually I need a room for at least another two nights. Maybe three – all depends," said Michael. He was attempting to discern when Tony's funeral might be held.

"Well then, welcome back. I think your room is ready for you."

"Your room, not a room," Michael mulled over what the desk clerk had said, and sure enough, he was given the key to the same room he had occupied the two previous evenings.

Michael was not hungry, so he decided to jot some notes in his journal. A lot had happened since his last entries the previous afternoon. "I especially need to log the events of last night, plus all what has gone on so far today," he said to himself.

Back in the hospital, after Michael left, Kathy and James went down to the hospital cafeteria for lunch. However, before selecting their food from the cafeteria, Kathy texted Darlene and John to tell them that the surgery had gone well and added, "Dad's been back in his room for a little while. James and I are going to get some lunch."

Kathy and James ate a light lunch and were soon headed back to Jake's room. As soon as they exited the elevator, they saw Ann Walden, their pastor from St. John's Church, leaving Jake's room. St. John's was the church home of all the Tollefsons for at least eight decades.

"Kathy and James, how are you both doing?" asked Pastor Ann.

"Fine Pastor Ann," Kathy replied for the two of them. "And how are you?"

"I'm doing well. And I am glad to see Jake's doing so well. He did, however, fall asleep on me during our prayer. I am sure he needs some sleep after all the excitement of last night and his surgery this morning. I'm guessing you two could use a little rest, too."

"I'll catch up on my rest when I get home," replied Kathy.

"Jake was so excited to tell me that Darlene is coming home. That's great. I hope you have a wonderful time," said Pastor Ann.

"We're all glad she is able to make it home."

"I'm happy for you. I have got to do a major presentation at a conference in Des Moines on Tuesday, so I will be gone from early tomorrow until Wednesday night. I'll try to check on you all sometime Thursday morning, if that's OK with you."

"That sounds just fine," replied Kathy.

It was fine with Kathy, but James was not so sure. He had a secret crush on his pastor and was hoping he would keep bumping into her the next couple of days when he was visiting his Dad at the hospital. He found himself wishing he were either ten years older, or back in confirmation class. For confirmation – sometimes called the pastor's class -- would allow him to see her more frequently.

Pastor Ann said so long, and Kathy and James stepped inside Jake's room.

While Jake snoozed the afternoon away, Kathy pulled out a large canvas bag containing some crocheting she had brought with her. James, who had purchased a Sunday edition of the Wisconsin State Journal in the lobby on their way back from the cafeteria, lifted out the sports section. After reading it, he reached over and retrieved the remote from Jake's hand and turned on a NASCAR race. It was not long, and Jake was not the only Tollefson who was sawing logs. James had joined his father.

Mid Sunday Afternoon

Tony's death was attributed to massive internal injuries and severe head trauma. It had not yet been determined if his accident was a suicide. Except for his ICU nurse, Tony was alone when he died. Tony had only two visitors during his hours in the ICU: Jake, who had stopped by Tony's cubicle on his way to surgery, and. his boss from the Chevy dealership – Ed Duncan. He had stopped to see Tony shortly after Jake's brief visit.

With Tony's stepfather in prison and having no known family members, Storm Blocker – the funeral director – called Ed to make the arrangements for Tony's funeral and burial. At their 2 P.M. meeting, Ed said: "Let's keep the whole thing rather simple."

Since the funeral home already had memorial services scheduled for Wednesday and Thursday, Storm suggested: "Since Tony's service will more than likely be rather small, it could be done as early as Tuesday afternoon." Ed concurred with Storm. The funeral was set for Tuesday at 2 P.M. An hour of visitation would precede the service.

Pastor Ann – who did nearly all the funerals for the "non-churched" of the community – and Tony was classified as one of these – would be asked to officiate at the service. And following the service, Tony's body would be cremated. Ed would receive the cremains.

There was however, one hitch in the plans. Pastor Ann was scheduled to be out of the state on Monday, Tuesday and Wednesday. She had been asked and agreed to do a major presentation on "The Relevancy of the Rural Church in 21st. Century America" at a conference on rural/small town ministry. "It's something that I really can't get out of," she indicated to Storm when he called her to see if she could conduct the service. Pastor Ann had prepared extensively for the conference – and "truth be told" – she did not want to cancel her presentation.

However, after she told Storm she would not be available, Pastor Ann thought of something. "Wait a second," she told Storm, "You remember Darlene Tollefson – Kathy and Jake's daughter? While I was visiting Jake at the hospital earlier this afternoon, he told me that she is coming in later tonight to visit her folks."

Storm, knowing of the events of the previous evening and realizing the reason Jake was in the hospital was from being hit by Tony, cautiously said to Pastor Ann: "Go on."

Pastor Ann continued: "Darlene might be able to do the service. You might recall, she was ordained five or six years ago, served a parish in Minnesota and is now back in graduate school, working on her doctorate. I heard that she has taken the summer off from her doctoral studies to be a chaplain in one of the national parks. I believe she is somewhere on the coast of Maine. But yes, she is coming home tonight. Maybe she would consider conducting the service. Since she grew up here, she might have known Tony. I am sure she has at least heard of him. I certain Darlene could do a good job."

"Thank you," said Storm. "I'll definitely check that out".

Immediately after speaking with Pastor Ann, Storm called the hospital. He requested to speak with someone at the nurse's station on the surgical unit. He assumed he could catch Kathy at the hospital. He asked the nurse in Jake's unit if Kathy was available. Kathy was in Jake's room, and the nurse who took Storm's call transferred him to Jake's room. Storm then asked Kathy for Darlene's cell phone number. Receiving it, he immediately called Darlene. Darlene was just about to board her plane in Bangor for a direct flight to Chicago. Storm explained the situation to her and said to Darlene, "With Tony being the one who hit your Dad and who punched your brother, you might not be inclined to do it, and I fully understand."

Yet with little hesitation, Darlene said: "Yes, I believe I can conduct the service. You said it is on Tuesday at 2 P.M. That will give me just enough time to prepare." A relieved Storm put down his phone and said: "Maybe this will somehow work out after all."

Having completed her conversation with Storm, Darlene slipped her cell phone into her carry-on bag. Almost immediately she thought: "What have I gotten myself into? What does one say at the funeral of the person who knocks out your brother, tries to kidnap your cousin, and then almost kills your father?" Although she had officiated at a couple dozen funerals during her four years as a pastor in Minnesota, this one would present a unique challenge. She would have to draw upon all her pastoral skills. And then she said to herself: "I really need to ask the good Lord for help in preparing and presenting Tony's service."

Then she remembered the guideline she often used when preparing for any public presentation. She needed to "T.H.I.N.K. First." That is, using the five letters of the word THINK as an acronym, she prayed that what she said would be true, helpful, inspirational, necessary, and kind. "Well, I've got a two-and-a-half-hour flight to Chicago. That will give me time to pray for the Lord's guidance," she said to herself as she prepared to board her plane.

Later Sunday Afternoon

Michael finished recording the events of his previous night and the past several hours. As he jotted his last note, he heard his stomach growl. It reminded him that he had skipped lunch in order to keep up with his paperwork. He decided to drive over the Jim's Diner once again. This was now the fifth time he had stopped there in the past two days. It was well into the afternoon and the restaurant's post-church crowd and noon-time rush was long over. Only a few tables were occupied. Michael made his way to his usual seat at the counter.

Betty, the same waitress who had served him during his previous visits to the Diner, handed him a menu – one filled with glossy pictures of entrees for breakfast, lunch and dinner. She said to him: "I thought you were leaving town this morning."

"I was," said Michael, "but then I realized I still might have a couple of things to tie up here."

"Well, welcome back. I'll be back to take your order in a minute or two."

Michael perused the menu that – by this time – had become quite familiar. He thought: "Well since it's Sunday, I suppose it's fried chicken; or better yet, how about some comfort food, like the meatloaf with mashed potatoes and green beans?" He decided on the later.

When Betty returned, he requested the meatloaf. He learned that it was one of the day's specials. And then he asked: "Can you top it off with a large milk?"

"White?" Betty asked.

"Yes," said Michael. "If you don't mind me asking, don't you ever leave this place?"

"Well, I'll tell you why that is. Jim's my husband. And you know what they say: 'If you own your own business, beware. It will own you.' Good thing the kids are grown up and out of the nest. We're never home."

"Now I understand," replied Michael.

As Betty left to place Michael's order with the chef, he caught a glimpse of several fresh pie options in a glass case on the wall behind the counter. "Looks like I might have to splurge and have some dessert today."

As he was awaiting his meal, Michael could not help himself from tuning into the conversation coming from three fellas sitting at a table immediately behind him. Michael picked up quickly that they were speaking about Tony and the events of the previous evening. "News sure travels quickly in a small town. It gets around even quicker with everyone on social media," mused Michael. He assumed the whole town must be hashing or re-hashing Tony's troubled life, the incident at Jerry and Nita's barn dance and the circumstances surrounding Tony's death.

As Michael listened, he was somewhat surprised by their comments. Michael began to bristle. "Guess he finally got what was coming to him," said one of the fellas. And then the other two piled on: "I say, good riddance. At least we won't have to worry about him beating up on our kids like he did to Jake and Kathy's boy just before he went out and killed himself." Michael thought: The assumption must be that Tony's death was a suicide. Then the fella seated immediately behind Michael took his shot: "Yes, we won't have to worry about that no-good punk anymore."

Michael had heard enough and felt he needed to say something to them. Swiveling his stool to face them, and then realizing he had seen them in the diner the previous evening, Michael said: "Excuse me, I couldn't help over-hearing your conversation concerning the Healy boy. From what I hear, it sounds like he didn't have much of a chance from the moment he was born."

"Are you saying you know him?" asked one of the trio.

"Didn't until last night when he walked in the Nelson's barn dance. That's when I learned about him and his background. Seems like it was tough going for him all along."

The youngest of the three responded: "I suppose you're right. He did have it pretty tough. Say, if you were at Nelson's barn dance, you probably saw everything that happened."

"Not really. I was still in the barn when all the action took place outside. The last I saw was Tony being dragged out of the barn by a couple of good-sized fellas. Tony was being a nuisance. He had been demanding beer and when he gave Jerry a shove, that's when these guys took action."

"Sounds like 'good ol' Tony," one of them said sarcastically.

"But I didn't see what happened after the guys dragged him out of the barn. By the time I got outside, Tony had already sped away."

Then, already knowing the answer for he had seen the same trio pull into Jack's parking lot the previous day, Michael asked: "Does that new Silverado belong to one of you?"

"Yes, it's mine," proudly said the oldest of the three. "What makes you ask?"

"Well, it's a pretty sharp vehicle. Did you get it here in town?"

"Thank you. Yes, I did; got it from Ed over at the Chevy dealership."

"And that pinstripe down the sides sure sets it off nicely." said Michael.

"It sure does," replied the proud owner with his two companions nodding in agreement.

"Did it come that way?" asked Michael.

"No; they added that at the dealership when it came in. Cost me an extra two hundred bucks, but I think it's worth it."

"Who did the work?" asked Michael.

"Come to think of it, I believe it was Tony," said the owner of the truck. "He does nice work; or I should say, he did nice work."

"I guess he was good at something." said Michael. "Oh, I see my lunch is here. I will not take up any more of your time. Nice visiting with you fellas."

Having said what, he felt he needed to say, Michael swiveled around, grabbed his fork, and took a bite of his meatloaf. "Oh my, almost as good as Elaine's," said Michael with a satisfied grin on his face.

Meanwhile, the three fellas at the table just behind him whispered to each other. Each asked the others if they knew the fella at the counter. They all shook their heads indicating they did not know him. But then the youngest reported to the other two: "Didn't we seen him in here last night?"

Sunday Night

Darlene pulled her Toyota Corolla rental car into her folk's long driveway. It was just before midnight. Stopping at the base of the front steps leading to the two-story prairie style farmhouse, she picked up her one suitcase, walked up the porch steps and rapped lightly on the front door. With no immediate response, she turned the doorknob and let herself in. It's kinda nice that there are still places where folks don't lock their doors, Darlene thought as she entered the front room of the home she had spent her childhood and most of her teenage years.

Kathy, who was awaiting her arrival, had fallen asleep on the sofa in the front room.

"Mom, I'm home," said Darlene just loud enough for Kathy to wake up, but not so loud as to startle her.

After awakening, Kathy rose from the sofa, gave Darlene a long hug, and reported: "I'm glad you could make it home, Honey. Your Dad and James will be glad to see you too. How was your trip?"

"Oh, not very eventful; but that's OK. Don't need any more excitement. Tell me, is there anything more about Dad? I got your text earlier saying that Dad's surgery went well. Just wondering how things are now. Any further updates?"

"Only thing I can say is your Dad slept most of the afternoon. Whenever he awakened he would ask when you were arriving. I had to keep reminding him that you would see him tomorrow. He was fine when I left him just before supper time. And he sounded even stronger when I called him about 8.

"Are you hungry? Want something to eat? I baked a couple dozen chocolate chip cookies yesterday morning. There should be plenty left; that is, if James hasn't devoured them."

"Thanks Mom, I think I'm going to pass on the cookies and hit the hay. It has been a full day and I'm bushed," said Darlene between yawns.

"I'm pretty exhausted, too," replied Kathy.

"Oh, Mom, before I go up, there's one thing I need to tell you: I heard about Tony Healy. Just before I got on the plane in Bangor, Storm Blocker from the funeral home called me and asked if I would officiate at Tony's funeral. Evidently Pastor Ann is going to be gone a few days and can't do it. I guess she told him that I might be available."

"And what did you say?"

"I told him that I would do it. I just don't know if I'm doing the right thing."

"First of all, Darlene, who do you think it was who gave Storm your cell number? And to answer your question: I don't think you've ever not done the right thing."

"Oh, Mom, there have been many times I've done the wrong thing. You just don't remember."

Kathy thought of something she felt Darlene needed to know: "Let me tell you what your Dad did as they were wheeling him to the surgical unit earlier this morning. He asked to stop to see Tony who was in the ICU. The attendant rolled up close to Tony, and your Dad said: 'I don't know if you can hear me, but I want you to know that I forgive you.'"

"Why am I not surprised? That sounds like something that Dad would do and say," responded Darlene.

"I'm proud that you agreed to do Tony's service, and your Dad will be, too. Again, you certainly are doing the right thing, Dear."

Darlene stood and reached down to pick up her suitcase. After saying "Good night, Mom," she turned and walked up the stairs to the second floor to her old bedroom.

"My," she whispered to herself. "It still looks the same after all these years. It's just the way I left it. So much has changed, but this room has not. Kind of nice." It made her feel like she was still her Mom and Dad's little girl. And it gave her a warm, cozy feeling as she slipped out of her traveling clothes and into her pj's.

Monday Morning

The morning seemed to come quickly for Kathy and Darlene. James was already up and busy with milking and other outside chores. Kathy and Darlene decided they would stop at Jim's Diner for a quick breakfast on the way to the hospital. Darlene had not been in the Diner for several years. She had a part-time job there during her junior and senior years of high school and was able to earn some spending money for college. Back then the diner was known as "Gramma's Kitchen" and operated by Jim's mother, Opal. A few years back, Opal passed away and Jim took over the business. He remodeled the place and gave it a new name: "Jim's Diner."

Jim questioned why he should change the name of an established business? But a trusted friend said to him: "You want more business? It's all about branding." So "Gramma's Kitchen" became "Jim's Diner." Along with the rebranding, Jim decorated the place with all sorts of mining equipment. And in a newly designed menu, the "house specials" were indicated by a small pickax just to the left of the listing. Two pickaxes meant the entree was not only a "special," but also a favorite "pick" of the diner's regular patrons.

As they approached the counter where they planned to sit, Kathy recognized the man seated at the far end of the counter. It was Michael.

Michael saw them and stood. Kathy said to him: "Michael, this our daughter Darlene; and Darlene, this is our friend, Michael."

Both Michael and Darlene acknowledged each other saying, "It's good to meet you."

Darlene, never known to be shy, said to Michael: "You're the one Mom was just telling me about on our drive into town.

She filled me in completely: How you met Dad in the mill on Saturday morning and ran into each other again at the Nelson's anniversary dance; how you brought Uncle Jack to the hospital Saturday night; how you waited to see how Dad was doing before you went to your motel; and how you were there yesterday when Dad got out of surgery. Thank you. Thank you for being with them through all this."

"Michael, have you decided how long you'll be staying with us in Platteville?" Kathy asked.

"I just overheard someone say that Tony's funeral is tomorrow. I think I will stay for that and then hit the road."

"Good, I'm glad to hear that you're staying."

"Michael, you probably haven't heard, but Darlene has been asked to officiate at Tony's funeral," Kathy informed Michael.

"From all I've been told about you, I am sure you'll do a fine job."

"Nothing Ike a little added pressure," Darlene answered.

"No. No pressure intended. Just meant it as a compliment and a word of encouragement," said Michael.

Then Michael asked, "How'd Jake get along during the night?"

Kathy replied: "I talked to him just before we left home. Sounded pretty chipper to me."

"Good to hear. Well, then you probably will not see me until later today. I'll be heading over to Mineral Point -- since I'm so close. I want to see if I can find some material for my students. I teach a semester of Wisconsin History and Culture each year. After I get back from Mineral Point, I'll try to stop by the hospital to see Jake."

"Don't feel like you have to. But I am sure Jake will be glad to see you," Kathy said.

"Oh, don't forget to top in Belmont. The Wisconsin Territory capital building is there," added Darlene.

"I see Betty's glancing this way. It looks like she's ready to wait on you. So, I best be on my way. Nice to meet you Darlene and good to see you again, Kathy," said Michael.

"So, we'll see you later then, Michael?" asked Kathy.

"You can count on it," said Michael. And having given his promise, Michael turned and walked toward the door, while Kathy and Darlene accepted menus from Betty.

They both ordered a waffle and coffee. This caused Darlene to remember "Waffle Houses." She reminded her mother: "Remember the first time you came down to see me at Vanderbilt. You said there must be a Waffle House at every exit along the interstate. You started counting them, but then lost track."

Kathy smiled at the memory.

When Kathy and Darlene finished eating they went to see Jake at the hospital. Darlene had a good visit with her Mom and Dad. Darlene told her folks about her summer position with "A Christian Ministry in the National Parks." Then she reported to them that having passed what she called her "qualifying exams," she was about to begin her dissertation. And then she talked about Craig – a fourth year medical student at Vanderbilt -- whom she had been dating for a couple of months. She flashed a broad smile as she told her folks he planned to see her in Maine in late July. "Best of all," Darlene said, "Craig is a Yooper – born and raised near Escanaba. And he hopes to return to the Upper Peninsula to practice family medicine when he's through with his internship and residency."

Then it was Jake's turn to speak to his daughter. He reviewed the events of Saturday – meeting Michael in the morning at the mill, the Barn Dance, the run-in with Tony's truck as he called it, and concluding with his reconciliation with Jack. "You know, if it took this run in with Tony to get Jack and I back together, then it's all worth it. And you, Darlene, being here makes it all even better."

Upon arriving in Mineral Point, Michael stopped at the Visitors Center. He opened a brochure that offered a brief history of the community and a list of places to visit. He was reminded that this part of the state was known as the "driftless" region. Untouched by the glaciers, the region contained minerals that were easily accessible.

Thus, Mineral Point became a center for the lead mining industry that had flourished in the region nearly two hundred years ago. It would take another several decades for dairy farming to become established not only around Mineral Point, but through the state. Michael read that many of the miners came to the area from Cornwall, England. They brought with them a special recipe for something called a pasty. The young woman seated at a desk in the visitors center told him: "You ought to try one. It is a pocket of pie-like crust filled with meat, rutabagas and potatoes. This was a meal that the miners could easily take to work with them." Michael wondered if these are like the pasties found in Upper Michigan, knowing that they, too, were a legacy of the miners that had labored there.

Michael also learned that when Henry Dodge was inaugurated as the first governor of the newly formed Wisconsin Territory on Independence Day of 1836, the event took place in downtown Mineral Point. And he noted that historians claim that for over a decade the lead-mining country controlled Territorial Wisconsin, and the politics of Mineral Point controlled the mining country. However, when the California Gold Rush occurred in 1849, many people left Mineral Point.

Michael walked toward downtown. He noticed that Mineral Point boasted a variety of artisans and craftspeople. Since Elaine collected pottery, he decided to stop at a few pottery shops. He found a matching set of chalices in the third shop. "Just what we need for a little wine before bedtime," he said to the potter. Then he added: "Now if I only can acquire a taste for it."

Michael walked through about a half dozen other shops before he decided he would go for an early lunch. His light breakfast -- a doughnut and orange juice -- was long gone.

He recalled that when he entered town and drove down its main street, he had spotted a restaurant with a large rooster above its door. He returned to the location, walked into the restaurant, and immediately saw a signboard that listed the day's specials. A pasty – the miners' fare – was among them. He remembered the recommendation of the woman at the Visitors Center: "You should try one."

"When in Rome, do as the Romans," Michael said to himself as he took a seat at the counter. He did not even have to look at the menu. "I'll take a pasty," he told the waitress.

Another of Wisconsin's many ethnic foods; this one gratis the folks from Cornwall, he thought. He questioned whether Wisconsin's general obesity was related not only to its consumption of beer, but also due to its many tasty ethic foods.

As Michael waited for his lunch, he recalled that his boyhood pastor had been born in Cornwall and had immigrated to the United States in the 1930's. Having eaten pasties during his childhood and youth, Rev. Tom missed them after coming to the States. So, on one of his trips back to England, he bought a pasty. He returned home with the pasty so that his wife could dissect it, and then attempt to make one. She was successful and she and Rev. Tom continued to enjoy them for several years.

When Michael's pasty arrived, he found it to be rather tasty, but somewhat dry. "Here, try this" encouraged the fella sitting on a stool next to him, handing Michael a bottle of ketchup.

"Thanks," said Michael

Michael poured out a mound of ketchup. Then filling his fork with his entree, he dipped it in the ketchup. "Ah, that's the trick," he said to himself as he continued to eat the entire pasty. Along with the pasty, he finished off a half bottle of ketchup.

After lunch Michael stopped at an extremely old settlement at the edge of town called Pendarvis. Here some of the town's original buildings -- dating back to the mining days -- were being preserved.

While there, one of the guides said something that Michael never failed to teach his Wisconsin History and Culture class: The derivation of the term "Wisconsin Badgers." It's not what many people think. It's not that Wisconsin has an abundance of this feisty stripped mammal. Rather, Wisconsin residents are called Badgers in recognition of those miners of the early 19th century who flocked to the mining region and lived in crude temporary shelters resembling badger holes.

Wanting to stop in Belmont on his way back to Platteville, Michael left Mineral Point by mid-afternoon. As he drove, he could not help but see the two large hills that stood out from the plains surrounding them. He had continued to see them each time he opened the door of his motel room and looked to the north. "So that's why the motel is called the Hillview. Makes sense," Michael mumbled to himself. He had noted that on the west side of the larger of the two hills was a large white letter "M" that stretched from near the crest of the hill to its base. After his visit to Mineral Point, Michael assumed: "Must stand for the early miners." He wondered how many of the area high school athletic teams were known as the "Miners." He was somewhat disappointed to learn that the teams at the university in Platteville were not called "Miners," but "Pioneers." He then conceded that many of the early pioneers were probably miners.

Soon Michael was in Belmont. Before Wisconsin became a state in 1848, Belmont had been the capital of the Wisconsin Territory. He was pleased to tour the white frame structure that served as the capital building. Certainly not near in size to the massive structure in Madison that so closely resembles the United States capital in Washington, D.C., he thought.

Michael picked up a large fold-out timeline of Wisconsin history. He thought: This will be great for my class. I wonder if I can scale it down and make a copy for each of my students. I suppose I'll have to get permission from the State Historical Society, but that shouldn't be a problem."

Monday Afternoon

Rather than returning to the hospital in the afternoon, Darlene thought she needed to spend some time in preparation for Tony's funeral. She was glad to have spent significant time in prayer during her flight to Chicago, asking for guidance regarding Tony's funeral.

Darlene was led to two texts: One from the sixth chapter of Micah and the other from Paul's letter to the Colossians. Her time was quite productive. Sitting at a small desk in her former bedroom, she was able to nearly complete her preparations by the end of the afternoon.

Monday Evening

Michael's plan was to see Jake after a light supper at Jim's Diner. With the pasty still being digested, Michael did not feel like a big dinner. Betty smiled and said as she served him a "Kid's Miner Burger" and side of cottage cheese: "With this meal you are officially a regular." He smiled and said: "Well, you probably won't see me after tomorrow. I'll be leaving town right after the Healy boy's funeral."

"Well, we're gonna miss seeing you," replied Betty.

Michael arrived at the hospital and made his way to Room 237. Jake was glad to see Michael. Michael did not know that Jake had slept for a good portion of the afternoon and feeling rested, Jake was eager to talk. Their discussion turned to farming and the changes that had been occurring in the dairy industry. Jake said, "The other day at the mill we were talking about changes on the farm..."

"Yes," said Michael.

"'I thought of another change. Back in the 60's and 70's, everybody wanted to be a Grade A farmer with their milk going into homogenized, pasteurized grade A milk. Those of us who became grade A milk producers received a little more per hundred. But now, most of our cows are producing milk that goes into cheese. And speaking of cheese, none of that processed stuff. The milk from a lot of the farmers around here is going to what are called artisan cheese factories. They make a lot of specialty cheeses. I bet your never heard of cranberry Gouda or dill Havarti."

Good, thought Michael, I am getting back on track and learning more about the changes in Wisconsin's dairy industry.

The two talked some more about their families. Jake was eager to report that Jack had helped James with the milking the past two days. "Our mother used to say, 'Let bygones be bygones.' I am so glad we have broken down that invisible wall that had separated us. But I keep thinking maybe I could have done more, so that we could have fixed our relationship sooner," said Jake.

"I don't know if you could have. I don't know if Jack would have been ready," replied Michael.

"You're probably right. But we sure wasted a lot of time. There is so much that we could have been doing together: not only farm work, but ballgames, picnics or just shooting the breeze. But like they say: 'Better late than never.'"

Then Jake added: "Dr. Glaser doesn't think this will leave me with a limp. I guess folks will still be able to tell who's Jack and who's me."

Michael could tell their conversation was winding down and he knew he wanted to record his days activities and so he said to Jake: "'I should be going; I've got a few things I need to do before calling it a day. I'll be leaving tomorrow right after Tony's funeral."

"Well Michael, it's been a real pleasure getting to know you."

"The pleasure's been mine," replied Michael.

"Do come this way again sometime; and when you do, bring Elaine. We'll do a cookout, or we'll all go over to Jim's Diner. I hear you've become a regular."

"Sounds like a wonderful idea, Jake."

Michael approached Jake's bed and reached out with both hands for a two-handed handshake.

"So long, until we meet again," said Jake. "And thanks for everything."

"You're welcome, Jake. Maybe I just happened to be in the right place at the right time."

"'Whatever, you've been like an angel to us."

Michael felt a little embarrassed but replied: "Thank you for your kind words. Goodbye then, Jake." Michael turned toward the door. A second later he looked back to address Jake: "I'll be thinking about you hoping your recovery goes fine."

"Thank you, buddy."

Michael turned again and walked out the door, while Jake said to himself: "There's one good fella. I bet his students are glad to have him."

A few minutes later Jake's nurse was in with his night-time meds. He took them and within five minutes he was sound asleep.

Meanwhile Michael made his way back to the Hillview Lodge. "Four nights in a row – at the same place, in the same bed. I would never have imagined," said Michael as he pulled in.

Tuesday Afternoon

Michael was relieved to remember that he had packed a pair of dress slacks, a button-down shirt, necktie and a pair of dress shoes. He could wear this ensemble and not feel under dressed for Tony's funeral.

Ed Duncan requested that Tony's casket be closed prior to the visitation. The trauma to Tony's body, including his face, was extensive. Ed said: "He just doesn't look like Tony. Let's have the casket closed for the whole proceedings." Before the visitation began, Ed placed a recent photograph of Tony on a table just to the left of Tony's casket.

The hour of visitation immediately prior to the funeral was more than enough time for the few who came to offer condolences. The only one receiving those condolences was Ed. Tony's stepdad, who was in prison for the aggravated assault and battery charge, had been notified of Tony's death. Upon hearing the news, Tony's stepdad's only comment was: "Why am I not surprised?" Tony's stepdad made no attempt to get a pass to attend the funeral.

Knowing Tony's reputation, Michael was not surprised to see that only about fifteen folks had shown up for the funeral. Michael joined Kathy and James, Jack, Mary and Angie in the second row. Across the aisle from them was Ed Duncan. Seated with him were four other employees from the Chevy dealership – three service technicians from the shop and the bookkeeper. Seated behind Michael and the five Tollefsons was a group of five folks from St. John's Church. They had watched Darlene grow up and wanted to see her in action – leading a worship service – something they had long awaited. Seated behind the group from St. John's was Cliff Engelbretson. Judy Waller – the woman who was with Cliff when Michael last saw him at the barn dance – was seated next to Cliff. And arriving just a moment before the start of the service and sitting in the back row were three fellas. Taking their seats just seconds before the start of the service, they had not yet arrived when Michael had surveyed the room.

Tony's funeral began as planned at 2 P.M. Darlene began with several reassuring Bible passages, ending with a reading of the 23rd Palm. She invited those who knew it "by heart" to say it along with her. She continued with a prayer and then read two additional Biblical texts: one from the prophet Micah and the other from Paul's letter to the Colossians – the readings she felt led to the previous day. As she finished the readings she nodded to Storm who then inserted a C.D. The reassuring words of "Amazing Grace" filled the chapel while Darlene took a seat behind the lectern.

After the song's concluding words Darlene stood to begin her meditation. She offered her first thought, saying that there are mysteries that come our way in life – some pleasant and some unpleasant or even tragic. But amid them all, she indicated, we are sustained by the mysteries of our faith. Among them is the assurance of a loving and forgiving God. She continued with a review of Tony's rather short life and premature death. She neither condemned him nor did she praise him, but openly noted the exceedingly difficult circumstances of his childhood and youth. Then Darlene indicated that it was not yet determined if Tony's death was a suicide. "But if it was," she said, "It is not ours to judge him, but to entrust him to a benevolent and forgiving God." She sought to be as truthful and gentle as she could, praying that the words she was speaking would offer hope and comfort to those attending the service.

As Darlene neared the completion of her meditation, she began to show some emotion as she continued: "I need to tell you that I am a fortunate young woman. Most of you know my Mom and Dad – Jake and Kathy Tollefson – good people and wonderful parents. I also have two great brothers – John who is in the Air Force and James who is here today. Some of you know that I am enrolled in a doctoral program at an outstanding university. Not everybody gets those kinds of opportunities. Tony certainly did not.

"My field of study is ethics. Ethics seeks to determine an answer to the question: What is good? That is why sometimes you hear folks asking: 'What is the ethical decision regarding a particular question or circumstance?' I have always been led by the prophet Micah in this endeavor, for offers a definition of the good when he proclaimed: 'What is good and what does the Lord require of us, but to do justice, love kindness and walk humbly with God.' Yes, I am thankful for Micah who informs us what is good. But I am also grateful for those who show us what is good. They are those who have -- as St. Paul wrote to the Colossians: 'Clothed themselves with compassion, kindnesses, humility, meekness and patience.' Moreover, they 'bear with one another and forgive each other just as the Lord has forgiven them.' Notice that Paul does not say they 'forgive and forget,' but 'forgive and forbear.' What does it mean to bear with each other? I like how someone described it to me, saying: 'As we are putting up with some other person's little idiosyncrasies, they are bearing with us and ours.'

"In my studies I have been learning a lot about ethics and pursuing the good. But I have discovered that the truly wise and faithful not only tell us what is good – they show us what is good. I know a man who recently showed such goodness – such kindness – such forgiveness: My Dad. Dad offered such forgiveness to Tony just before Dad went into the operating room for his surgery. It was shortly before Tony died. With all my learning about ethics and determining what is good, nothing has impacted me as much as those truly wise and faithful ones who have shown me what is good. My hope is that we will go from this place inspired by such examples, and possessing a willingness to forgive, just as we have been forgiven by our Lord."

Darlene then offered a closing prayer which led into the Lord's Prayer. Many of the attendees joined her in praying the well-known words.

After the "Amen," Darlene took her place alongside of Tony's casket. She offered the commendation. She used the exact same words she had spoken for every funeral or memorial service she had ever done – except for changing the name of the deceased: "Into your hands O merciful Savior, we commend your child, Tony. Acknowledge we humbly pray, a sheep of your own fold, a lamb of your own flock and a son of your own redeeming. Receive him into the arms of your mercy, into the blessed rest of everlasting peace, and into the company of the saints of light. Amen."

At the Close of the Funeral

Darlene then moved to the left of the table that held Tony's picture as Storm inserted a C.D. containing the recessional music. Then Storm slowly walked down the center aisle. He appeared to be ready to dismiss those in attendance. That's when Ed jumped up from his seat on the aisle and walked briskly to the casket, leaned on it and cried out: "Tony, Tony, my son; can you ever forgive me?" The sound of Ed's sobs filled the room as he continued his confession: "O Tony, you were so lost; and for so much of it, I blame myself. O God, have mercy on me."

Had the mystery of nearly twenty years been solved? Was Ed Duncan Tony's birth father?

Jack Tollefson – who had purchased vehicles from Ed for nearly thirty years stepped forward from his spot at the far end of the second row and rushed forward to comfort his friend. He put an arm around Ed's trembling body. Then Jack spoke softly to Ed: "I couldn't help hearing what you said. Let me tell you what a friend told me when I wondered if the Lord would forgive me. He said: 'If the Lord forgave those who were about to nail him to the cross, I think he can forgive you, too.'" Ed turned toward Jack and the two embraced, while the others who had attended the funeral began to make their way to the exit.

Michael, watching what had just transpired, remembered that Kathy had called him an angel when she introduced him to Dr. Glaser on Sunday. Jake too, had suggested he was an angel. Then Michael considered: Maybe there are angels all around us, appearing to us when we need them the most. It's just that they do not have wings; they are sometimes in disguise. They might even be dressed in suit clothes – like Jack Tollefson.

After Michael said his good-byes to the Tollefsons – the second time in a little over two days -- he turned toward his pickup. As he did, he heard a voice calling out. This was not one of his nudges. It was a loud audible voice coming from somewhere in the parking lot. "Hey, hey you, wait a minute." Michael sensed the words were being directed toward him. He turned and noticed three fellas walking in his direction. They were the same three that he had seen and talked to in Jim's Diner on Sunday afternoon. Michael had not noticed them sitting in the last row of the funeral home because they had not arrived when Michael had inventoried the small congregation.

The trio approached Michael and the spokesman for the group – the oldest and the one who owned the new Silverado – said: "After you talked with us at the diner on Sunday afternoon, we decided the least we could do for Tony was to come today and pay our respects."

All three reached out to shake hands with Michael. Then they made their way to the new Silverado with the pinstripe that Tony had installed.

Michael turned, walked toward his red Ford pickup and thought: "I guess I really was supposed to come back here for a couple more days. Now, maybe I can get to the Mississippi River and possibly on to Lacrosse before it gets dark."

. .

www.ingramcontent.com/pod-product-compliance
Lightning Source LLC
Chambersburg PA
CBHW052113110526
44592CB00013B/1594